*of transition, and the awareness that the examples they set day-to-day have a huge impact on company-wide ethical conduct."*

—MAHENDRA GUPTA, DEAN, OLIN BUSINESS SCHOOL,
WASHINGTON UNIVERSITY IN ST. LOUIS

*"Harlan Steinbaum has done a masterful job of assembling a collection of very personal vignettes written by CEOs regarding a pivotal moment in their careers. Whether you are or have been with a very large corporation or a much smaller company or somewhere in between, or you are at the beginning, the middle, or the end of your career, there is something in this book for you."*

—JAMES M. DENNY, LEAD DIRECTOR, AND FORMER CEO
GILEAD SCIENCES, FORMER VICE CHAIRMAN, SEARS ROEBUCK

*"I believe that Harlan Steinbaum's book is powerful and important reading for anyone seeking to be successful in a world where people skills and ethics are critical."*

—AL GOLDMAN, CHIEF STOCK MARKET STRATEGIST FOR FORTY-
EIGHT YEARS, A. G. EDWARDS

*"Harlan Steinbaum gives us a privileged perspective on 'the' moment in the lives of remarkable business leaders that, as they tell us, defined their careers and lives. The autobiographies are written as a series of snapshots across a panorama filled with executives from many industries and with diverse backgrounds regarding their education, gender, race, and beliefs. The common link is the importance of the human bond, be it mentor, a parent, or best friend. The book is a grounded analysis of leadership as defined by the necessity to decide, to take the decision and the risk, and then make the best of it. An engaging book that provides substantial value to the reader."*

—BRUCE KOGUT, SANFORD C. BERNSTEIN PROFESSOR OF
LEADERSHIP AND ETHICS, COLUMBIA BUSINESS SCHOOL,
COLUMBIA UNIVERSITY

*"The experiences and insights shared in* Tough Calls from the Corner Office *are as meaningful to leaders of not-for-profit organizations as they are to executives of profit enterprises. Developing successful philanthropic organizations requires creating an organizational culture, recognition of opportunities, decision making, and leadership. Harlan Steinbaum has presented examples of these important issues drawn from the experiences of business leaders and has created a fascinating read."*

—MARYLEN MANN, FOUNDER AND
CHAIRMAN OF THE BOARD, OASIS INSTITUTE
(A NOT-FOR-PROFIT ORGANIZATION OF 360,000 MEMBERS)

# Tough Calls *from the*
## CORNER OFFICE

# Tough Calls *from the* CORNER OFFICE

TOP BUSINESS LEADERS REVEAL
THEIR CAREER-DEFINING MOMENTS

## Harlan Steinbaum

with Dave Conti and Michael Steinbaum

HARPER
BUSINESS

*An Imprint of* HarperCollins*Publishers*
www.harpercollins.com

HarperCollins books may be purchased for educational, business, or sales
promotional use. For information, please write: Special Markets Department, HarperCollins Publishers, 10 East 53rd Street, New York, NY 10022.

FIRST EDITION

*Designed by Cassandra J. Pappas*

Library of Congress Cataloging-in-Publication Data has been applied for.

ISBN 978-0-06-180249-2

11 12 13 14 15    OV/RRD    10 9 8 7 6 5 4 3 2 1

# Contents

# Tough Calls *from the*
# CORNER OFFICE

# Introduction

What if you could have private conversations with some of the top executives and business builders in the country? What if you could sit down with them and discuss the most important decisions of their careers, the moments that made them what they are, the catalysts that pushed their companies to the pinnacle of success and created their legacies for all time? Imagine what you would learn: the lessons, principles, strategies, ideas, and solutions to all the business issues you might encounter in a lifetime.

I decided to do just that. I reached out to some of the most successful and respected businesspeople in corporate America—leaders from companies such as Verizon, Chrysler, McDonnell Douglas (now part of Boeing), ESPN, Ogilvy & Mather, A. G. Edwards (now part of Wells Fargo), Fleishman-Hillard, Enterprise Rent-A-Car, WellPoint, and Panera Bread Company. The results are in your hands: a treasure trove of rich business wisdom, stories of tough decisions and hard-won victories, and lessons from lifetimes of achievement.

My name is Harlan Steinbaum, and I am a former CEO.

In looking back over my own career in business, I realized that among the many choices and decisions I had made, there was one that stood out above all the rest in terms of its impact on my company, my career, my family, and my subsequent success.

It was the moment when my brothers-in-law and I decided to buy back the family business from the conglomerate that had purchased it from us several years earlier—and to run it ourselves once again. That decision, and the actions that flowed from it, came to define me and my life in business. My life would never be the same because of that decision. It was the gateway to my future. It was my defining moment.

Over the years I've become fascinated with these career-defining points in time, not only because they are so often interesting and dramatic as stories in and of themselves, but also because they have so much to teach us.

A defining moment, I have found, isn't always the decision that makes the most money for the company or the person. Years after buying back the family business, we founded a very successful joint venture called Express Scripts. Yet, in looking back, I don't find that that decision or the resulting enterprise, as successful as it was, really defined me professionally.

In my view, a defining moment is the decision or action a person takes that has the greatest impact on his or her career. It's a moment that shapes us as individuals and as businesspeople and sets the trajectory for the events that follow. It doesn't necessarily have a positive short-term outcome. Sometimes our most significant learning experiences come from our failures, not our successes.

Many of us won't know our defining moment until we reflect on our careers after the passage of time to see how certain events, decisions, and judgments played out—when we can measure their effect on us and our work. That's how it was for me. Even after many years, I can still clearly see my own defining moment. It began with my restlessness and dissatisfaction with the status quo and my desire to take greater control of my future.

My defining moment starts with a company called Medicare-Glaser Corporation, a retail chain of drugstores and pharmacies. The company was founded by my father-in-law, Morris Glaser, in 1923. (By the way, we had nothing to do with the U.S. government's Medicare program, and in fact we had the name before that program was created.) At one point we owned stores in Missouri, Illinois, Connecticut, Tennessee, and New York. In all, we owned and operated over one hundred stores. As the company grew, we became the first drug chain to open its own chain of stand-alone retail pharmacies, with a focus on dispensing discounted prescriptions. Its purpose was to help the many people who could not afford the cost of their medications.

In 1970 I became president of the Glaser Drug Stores and Medicare Pharmacies. Soon after, we began to consider an initial public offering to provide additional capital to grow the business. In 1972, while these discussions were taking place, we were contacted by Pet, Inc., a diversified conglomerate listed on the New York Stock Exchange. Pet was interested in acquiring us. After months of discussions, we decided to make a deal and become a division of Pet.

When Pet first became interested in purchasing our drugstore chain, we were enthralled by the prospects. Pet's plan was to grow the chain into a nationwide competitor. With its resources, we could expand both organically and through acquisition on a scale we had never dreamed of before, and we could then really compete with the big boys in our industry.

I was tired of seeing a Walgreen's open up across the street from virtually every store we opened. Walgreen's, with its size and sheer buying power, would lower prices on key products to get people in its doors. It could sustain lower prices much longer than we could. As a result, we had to be more innovative than Walgreen's to keep our customers from going across the street. Now, as part of Pet, we would finally play ball with Walgreen's on a more level playing field.

Once our company became integrated into Pet, I became a group president with profit-and-loss responsibility for six out of its seventeen operating divisions. From that vantage point, I gained a better view of company management and philosophy and came to realize that Pet was weighted down by some classic "big company" structures and thinking. The company moved slowly, people deliberated about deliberating, and good old-fashioned entrepreneurial-style risk-taking was avoided, not courted. When challenges arose, the pattern and practice was to take the path of least resistance. On one occasion, Pet's supermarket customers, who represented an important part of its distribution base, were complaining because our drugstores and liquor stores, which I also managed, were taking high-margin business from them. They threatened to stop buying some grocery products from Pet in retaliation. In response, Pet slowed the growth of the drugstores and liquor stores.

In general, a premium seemed to be placed on managing problems rather than solving them. I didn't have confidence that in the long run this was good practice, and I simply didn't want this type of culture to dictate my future or that of my family or my company. My original partners and I became convinced that we could grow the company smartly by being nimble and taking the right risks, even though we wouldn't have the same resources to draw upon. As with most business decisions, there were pros and cons on both sides, but in the end we felt strongly about retaking control of our destiny.

We decided to approach Pet management and try to reacquire our company. After a lot of surprised reactions, followed by some tough negotiations, we arranged a leveraged buyout. We had won our company back, but not without taking on a lot of debt.

Although I felt that this was the right decision for me and my company, I don't want to leave the impression that Pet itself seemed like a lost cause to me—far from it. Like any successful company, it did a lot of things right and was rewarded for it. We learned a lot from our Pet years that we were able to put to good use. It was a professionally managed company with a lot of good people, and its management sophistication rubbed off on us, giving us an advantage that few other companies our size had. As a result, our newly reacquired company was blessed with both an entrepreneurial spirit and professional management. This is a rare combination.

With our destiny back in our own hands, we built a unique and dynamic company. We continued to grow, opening a chain of low-cost prescription vision center stores as well as developing other retail concepts. In time, we had an initial public offering that provided us with growth capital.

We transformed ourselves and our firm into leaders in the retail drug industry. Some of our moves transformed the industry itself. For example, we developed the first chemically based drug interaction database used by pharmacists to alert them to potential drug-to-drug or drug-to-food reactions. Then, in the late 1980s, we became the first in our industry to open a health care center in one of our pharmacies. We began to fill mail-order prescriptions, and the business continued to grow.

We also started a joint venture with one of our business partners. The new company, called Express Scripts, was a pharmacy benefit management business that included prescription fulfillment through the mail. I was its first chairman. I'm proud to say that the company now serves the prescription drug needs of over 50 million Americans. Express Scripts has grown into a Fortune 500 company.

All of these events are a direct or indirect result of my defining moment, which put me on a path that I can look back on with satisfaction. It also taught me some important lessons.

I learned to have the intellectual honesty to face problems head-on—not rationalize them away or try merely to manage them, but to get to the sources or causes and then figure out a way to eliminate them.

I learned that hiring the best people pays off.

With cash flow tight, I learned to be careful and tough-minded when it came to management and planning. Only with great discipline and tight control could we have grown and prospered through the early, fragile years of the repurchased company.

I also learned that in business you never do anything alone. I had a long and interesting career, and at every step of the way I worked shoulder to shoulder with three wonderful people: my two brothers-in-law, Lou Glaser and Ralph Silversmith, and another executive, our CFO, Stuart Bascomb. Everything I did, I did with them. They were great partners, colleagues, advisers, and friends.

THE PERSONAL IMPACT that this one business decision—my defining moment—had on my life made me curious about other business leaders. I wondered whether others had experienced similar kinds of moments in their careers. To find out, I decided to contact top executives around the country and ask them.

The results were fascinating. In the course of their careers, these business leaders had made thousands of decisions, but most of them felt that there was indeed one decision that stood out above the rest. That decision had served as their crucible and made a profound impact on them both personally and professionally.

I've elected to have these executives tell the stories of their defining moments *in their own words*. In no other way could I capture the authenticity of their experiences, the depth of their knowledge, the knowing quality of their voices.

I've organized the book around the classic arc of a successful businessperson's career: early key career choices, risks and opportunities, working with partners, business transformations, and the final leave-taking from the world of work. I end the book with a special chapter on defining moments that transcend the typical concerns of business.

I've also assembled a great collection of business advice from these executives in an appendix called "Executive Advice and Wisdom." I asked them to provide an unconstrained list of advice, suggestions, and pointers—whatever they wanted to pass on to readers. The result is a document that, in my opinion, may be one of the more interesting lists in all of business.

I invite you now to sit down with these men and women, listen to their stories, absorb their wisdom, and learn.

# CHAPTER I

# The Road Taken:
# Making Key Career Choices

D efining moments often come during periods of transition, when the atmosphere is charged and the business environment is changing. It's at these times that leaders step forward and make their mark.

Another kind of transition, however, has little to do with company or business issues, but instead involves personal career issues. It's a defining moment that occurs when we look inward and begin to ask questions like: What do I really want out of my professional life? What are my goals? What's going to make me happy? This chapter and the next feature executives whose defining moments came out of such questions.

Few of us really know what our professional goals are from the start. None of the executives in this chapter—and just a handful in the rest of the book—had it figured out from the beginning. Stories of major changes in midstream or several changes over the course of a lifetime are the norm, not the exception.

As diverse as these stories are, an important common thread runs through them: at some point these people figured out what really made them tick, and they let that insight guide their decisions.

Some people find it easy to figure out what excites them professionally. In chapter 4, we'll see that Monty Hall, the famous game show host and producer, knew from the beginning that he wanted to be in the entertainment business. But for many of us the difficulty of getting to a useful and revealing analysis of our professional goals is separating what everyone—family, friends, society—tells us is important from what's actually important to us personally. There are a lot of red herrings out there, and sometimes it can take a while to figure out where our own true north lies.

Danny Meyer, the famous New York restaurateur, was about to pick his second (and possibly wrong) career because he never let himself entertain the idea of becoming a restaurateur. It was simply not the type of career to which an expensive liberal arts education usually led. A doctor or lawyer, yes. But not a restaurant owner. He had to admit to himself that he really wanted to be in the restaurant business, and then he had to have the strength to take an unconventional path that some in his family did not fully endorse.

The starting point for any career decision must be what a person knows about himself or herself. If prestige makes you tick, great. If you have to be in a creative pursuit, fine. If you know that you need a career where you can make discoveries or educate children or build something or work with animals or deal in rare books—fantastic. The key is to figure this out and make it part of your decision-making criteria.

For most of my career I was in the drugstore business; once my partners and I had established ourselves in the marketplace, we expanded into vision stores, hearing aid stores, and mail-order prescriptions. When I was at Pet, Inc., I had a diverse group of companies reporting to me: a liquor store chain, a label manufacturer, an upscale party center chain, a specialty and gourmet foods manufacturer, and a fireplace retailer. I'm sure there was something that tied these companies together, but I never found it.

The fact is that it never mattered to me what industry I was in because I love the process and challenge of business in general. To me, it's a multifaceted game. There's the financial game, the marketing game, the strategic game, the operations game, and the interpersonal game. I think I could have been happy in virtually any industry because I found each of these fundamental aspects of business exciting.

Of course, not everyone is fortunate enough to pick a career they love, but I believe that those who do will have a better chance at succeeding. Back to Danny Meyer—he was on track to become a lawyer, but decided not to. Good choice. It wasn't his passion. I know a lot of unhappy lawyers who are quietly looking around for something better suited to them. I also know a lot of happy lawyers who really love everything about their work—the thought process, the cases, the deals, the complexities. These lawyers love helping clients and love winning for them. You know who I want to be my lawyer when I need one? One of these people. Not one who would rather be a sports agent or a politician or a screenwriter. It's not that lawyers who are searching for their true passion are bad legal practitioners, but I want someone who is passionate about the law working on my case or my deal. That person—the lawyer who goes the extra mile—ultimately is the best counsel for his or her clients. When you love what you do, you can be passionate about it without faking it. As Joseph Plumeri, the CEO of Willis Group, told me, everyone wants to be around people with real passion.

There is one more common thread that runs through the stories in this book, especially those in chapter 1. None of these executives looked for an easy way out. All of them knew they were in for a lot of grueling work and long hours while they paid their dues.

When I started at Glaser Drug Company, I had come from real

estate. I knew little about the drugstore business and less about retail operations. I had no background in marketing, inventory management, pharmacy operations, product selection, and so on. I had to learn it all on the job. The first thing I did was get "into the field" so I could be exposed to all aspects of the business. I spent time at the cash register, in the warehouse, and behind the pharmacy counter. After I had been on the job for probably a month, I was working behind the pharmacy counter when a woman came up and asked for her prescription. I got the package and gave it to her. She took the package but gave me a suspicious glare. She kept looking at me and didn't walk away. Finally she blurted out, with no small sense of shock and a bit of horror, "Hey, I know you. Last month you sold me my house—and today you're filling my prescription?" I did know enough about retail customer relations to assure her that I hadn't actually filled the prescription but was simply handing her the package.

These kinds of stepping-stones in a career might not be the sexiest and most satisfying, but if they lead in the right direction, they provide valuable and necessary learning experiences. And since there are no shortcuts around them anyway, go ahead and embrace them.

I'm not suggesting that you can develop a career plan for yourself in the same way you would develop a business plan for your business, but there are some processes that can be taken from business planning that provide a model for moving forward and reacting to career situations.

It's as simple as setting goals, knowing your decision-making factors, and establishing priorities. This provides a starting point for assessing opportunities. For some people, the goal is money, regardless of how it's made. For others, the goal is attaining a lofty position or having a high level of responsibility in a specific field. Some people insist on doing interesting work, or working in a specific location, or achieving a healthy work-life balance. No one can tell you what your goals and priorities are (or how much sacrifice or risk you'll tolerate to achieve them), but they should be articulated and factored into every decision you make.

In this chapter, we see some far-reaching decisions that were made in the early part of a person's career, while others involved midcareer job offers that forced the issue. These weren't decisions based simply on where the most money or the most prestige could be earned. Each person looked at the totality of the opportunity and filtered that view with his or her personal decision-making factors. All of these executives seized an opportunity and gave it everything they had to make it a success. This kind of relentless effort—the final common element here—certainly has a way of covering for any deficiencies in the career script.

## DANNY MEYER
### CEO, Union Square Hospitality Group

Without Danny Meyer, New York would be a far less tasteful place. Meyer is the owner-operator of some of the city's most legendary eateries, including the beloved Union Square Café, the top-rated Gramercy Tavern, Tabla, Eleven Madison Park, Blue Smoke, and Shake Shack. As head of the Union Square Hospitality Group, he runs a group of highly regarded Manhattan restaurants that are visited by tens of thousands of discerning diners each year. Now that he has brought his cuisine and renowned hospitality to the New York Mets' new baseball park in Queens, his reach has extended into the outer boroughs of the city as well.

Meyer's career in the restaurant business almost didn't happen. It was almost a road not taken. As a young man out of college, he started in sales at a company that developed electronic article surveillance security systems. An offer from his employer to take on a bigger, more important role in the company forced him to make a tough decision: should he stay with this career and start moving up or should he move on? The situation was a turning point for Meyer, but he almost turned in the wrong direction!

Meyer struggled to make the right choice. He weighed his passion against more practical and typical career considerations. His emergence as one of the most successful restaurateurs in the world certainly validates his early decision and suggests to all of us that following one's heart is the surest way to a satisfying career.

———

THE JOB I had before opening my own restaurant was account manager for a company called Checkpoint Systems, which sold electronic tags to stop shoplifters. This was in the early 1980s. The company was based in a wonderful town called Thorofare, New Jersey, and I had the New York territory. I was their leading salesman for three consecutive years and was becoming a star, getting awards, trophies, free trips. Everything was working out nicely.

The company approached me about moving to London to help launch their product overseas. I was fascinated with the idea of living in London and being able to explore Europe. But instead of jumping at the opportunity, I had to admit to myself that this work was not my passion. Actually, I wasn't sure what my passion was. I had a degree in political science from Trinity College, and I had some thoughts about running for public office—becoming a politician.

I spent my entire youth fascinated with politics and had worked in it both professionally and as a volunteer. I worked for U.S. Senator Symington in Washington, D.C., one summer; I worked as the Cook County, Illinois, field coordinator for John Anderson's presidential campaign in 1980; and in 1977 I worked in the Connecticut State Legislature. Maybe it was time for me to go do it.

The London job offer forced my hand: I was either going to go forward with Checkpoint and the opportunity they were giving me, or I was going to stop doing the job altogether and move on.

I thought, *All right, here's your opportunity to see if politics is the way to go, and the way to figure it out is to become a lawyer first.* The traditional path to public office had always been to study law before running for a government office.

So I signed up to take the LSATs, the exam law schools look at to decide if they're going to accept you. Literally on the eve of taking my LSATs, I knew something was wrong with my decision.

Just before the day of the exams, I had dinner with my grandmother, who was in town from Chicago, as well as my aunt and uncle who live here in New York. I guess I was showing my confusion, because my uncle said, "What's wrong?" I blurted out, "I don't really want to be a lawyer."

He came back with, "Well, why don't you do what you've been talking about your whole life?"

"What's that?"

"All I've ever heard you talk about is restaurants. Why don't you become a restaurateur?"

It was true. I was always talking about restaurants, but back in 1984 it was just about unthinkable to parlay a liberal arts degree into a job in the restaurant business. It just wasn't a valid career choice. It certainly wasn't the kind of career you wanted to tell your parents that all of your education has led to.

Without any question, the defining moment in my career was realizing I had the courage to pursue restaurants as a career. It was from that night on that I felt completely relaxed about everything. I did take the LSATs; I think I did pretty well on them, but I didn't apply to even one law school.

The next day I picked up the phone and called a good friend from Trinity College and said, "Would you like to take a restaurant management course with me? We could open a restaurant together. You could be the money guy and I could be the food and wine guy."

At the time my friend was in a bank training program at US Trust. But without thinking too much about it, he said, "Sure. Let's do that." So we enrolled at the New York Restaurant School. A couple classes in, he admitted to me that it didn't feel right to him and that he was not going to continue. He ended up going to business school instead.

But he told me, "I feel badly about leaving you in the lurch. One of our clients at US Trust is in the restaurant business. Would you like me to introduce you? Maybe I could get you a job there." And so he introduced me, and sure enough, I got a $250-a-week job at a seafood restaurant called Pesca on East Twenty-second Street in New York.

I had given up a $120,000 job as an account manager for Checkpoint Systems to take a $250-a-week job as an assistant manager at a seafood restaurant in an unfamiliar neighborhood of New York. But I had to do it. It was like having an itch that if I didn't scratch I was going to go nuts. And not only did that choice introduce me to the career of my life, it also introduced me to Michael Romano, who also worked at Pesca. He later became my chef and partner at Union Square Café and all of our other businesses.

I never would have met Michael had it not been for taking that job at Pesca. I never would have met my career had it not been for that job. I never would have met the neighborhood in which most of my restaurants are located. And I would say, more important than everything, I never would have met my wife, Audrey, who was waiting tables there. She was an actress, and as so many actresses do, she was working as a waitress to earn a living between theater jobs and commercial work.

There was a lot of risk in pursuing my passion for the restaurant business. But I had to find out. It wasn't just the choice of giving up the career with Checkpoint, but it was also the choice of giving up the career in politics that I thought I had been pointing toward my entire life in order to pursue something that no one in my family really understood or embraced.

I talked to everybody in my family about my decision. The only one who really, really tried to talk me out of it was my maternal grandfather. But when things worked out for me, he acknowledged his mistake—and my success—with a smile. He got a big kick out of telling everybody how wrong he was.

## ANGELA F. BRALY
### President, CEO, and Chairman of the Board, WellPoint, Inc.

Angela Braly runs the largest health care company in the United States. Serving more than 34 million members, her company, WellPoint, Inc., is one of only two Fortune 35 companies with a female CEO.

Her success was not driven by the usual executive desire to make a run for the corporate brass ring. Rather, Braly's rise to the top had everything to do with wanting to achieve something meaningful in her life that would have a positive impact on people. She wanted to make a difference.

In fact, Braly never intended to ride the corporate merry-go-round at all. An attorney by trade, she entered the world of health care through an assignment to provide legal counsel to a not-for-profit Blue Cross and Blue Shield company that was converting to for-profit status.

Dry stuff. But she was drawn to the situation's legal complexities and then to the company's mission to provide health care security to everyday people. She saw what a vitally important factor health care could be in people's lives, and she was determined to get the legal work done right.

That work opened up a new opportunity that presented Braly with a classic fork in the road. One path led back to the familiar world of law; the other pointed toward an uncertain future in a business she was more and more convinced held great meaning for her. Which way to turn? The choice she made began her journey not only to extraordinary corporate success but also, more importantly, to a place where she felt she could make a difference in the world by contributing in a positive way to the well-being of millions of Americans.

———

I ALWAYS THOUGHT I would be a lawyer. I went to a terrific law school and was on the partnership track with a well-respected law firm in Missouri—Lewis, Rice & Fingersh.

At the firm, I served as outside counsel to several businesses. One of them was Blue Cross and Blue Shield of Missouri. I was brought in to resolve some legal disputes that had arisen due to their conversion from a not-for-profit to a for-profit company.

It was a complicated situation that took two years to settle. In the midst of our work, they asked me to join the company. I said, "I don't want to leave the law firm, but I'll be your interim general counsel." That way I could still remain with Lewis, Rice & Fingersh.

At the time, one of my mentors at the law firm told me, "Don't be gone from the firm for more than a year, because if you are, you'll lose the relationships you have with your clients. If you do that, it will be hard to come back."

I worked with Blue Cross and Blue Shield of Missouri for a year. It was coming on the one-year anniversary, and thinking back to what my mentor had said, I realized, *I've got to make a decision here, because my year is up.*

What challenged and inspired me was the complexity and importance of health care, especially the opportunity to do something very important—to provide people with health care security.

I thought to myself, *I need to do this because I am so committed to getting this right, and we're not done with our work. I have to get this right.* So I decided to stay. It really was the right thing to do.

That was the important career decision of my life.

There were risks with leaving a partner position in a prominent law firm, but that decision has put me on an amazing path leading an organization dedicated to improving the health of so many people and our communities.

The stakes were high. I was leaving a law firm where I had made partner to take on a role that I knew very little about. Serving as inside counsel is very different from serving as outside counsel. I was comfortable in my role at the law firm and knew what to expect. Leaving that comfort and becoming more involved with the business aspects of an organization created risks and opportunities. In the end, the draw of the opportunities and the challenge drove me to make this decision.

At first, the Missouri health plan was facing some pretty difficult challenges, and my role was to help management navigate those challenges, including the complex transition from not-for-profit to for-profit status. Fortunately, I was able to help the health plan successfully manage those issues and, along the way, create a billion-dollar charitable foundation. It was the second-largest medically related health care foundation in the United States, dedicated to improving health care access and overall health for the neediest people in the state.

My role today—leading WellPoint—grew out of that decision to become general counsel to the Missouri health plan. After becoming inside counsel, my role and responsibilities continued to grow and change. I was appointed the president of the Missouri health plan and subsequently served as general counsel for WellPoint, while also overseeing the company's public policy and communications efforts.

When I became president and CEO of WellPoint, I gained even greater insight and understanding into the day-to-day implications of every decision we make—and how our decisions affect our customers, our communities, and our company.

I follow three principles that have guided me for years. First, do the right thing. For me, this is gravity. It is at the core of everything we do. Second, do it for the customer. In meetings with our associates, I emphasize that our customers are the reason we're here. We want to provide them with the very best possible health care experience. And third, do it right the first time. I know that's not always possible, but our customers expect us to, and that is our goal. If we don't do it right the first time, we will improve our processes so that the next time we will.

I would like to be remembered as having positively impacted the quality of and access to health care in the United States. At WellPoint, we're developing programs and services that truly improve the health of our members—whether it is through innovative care management programs or through our public policy positions to drive responsible, sustainable reform. I do believe that collaboration between insurers, hospitals, doctors, business, and government will lead to an improved health care system in the United States—so that quality care is affordable and accessible to all.

# JAMES H. SPEED JR.
## President and CEO, North Carolina Mutual
## Life Insurance Company

---

James Speed had a plan. He wanted to be an accountant, and he knew the degrees he needed to gain entry into that profession. Although he had worked hard to earn them, he believed that it was going to be a problem that he had not gone to well-known schools for either college or graduate school.

The way Speed saw it, his problem was compounded by the fact that there were simply not many African Americans in the upper echelons of corporate finance departments, which was where he wanted to be.

After earning his MBA and spending a couple of years getting some corporate work under his belt at a large manufacturing firm, Speed was ready to plunge into the job market again. Multiple offers came in, and he found himself at a crossroads. One road led to the kind of corporate work he had always aspired to, with a great salary and all the perks. The other was lower-paying and promised a lot of hard work, blood, sweat, and tears.

The choice he made created a solid foundation for the rest of his career. It helped him overcome what he had believed were the major obstacles to his ability to rise to the top. And his choice eventually led to his elevation to the presidency of North Carolina Mutual, the largest African American—owned life insurance company in the United States.

Speed's path to the executive suite was not a direct one. In midcareer, he made an important life-changing decision when he left the corporate world to spend more time with his daughter, who was then a sophomore in high school. He didn't want to miss this time in his daughter's life. He went to all of her sports events, traveled to Europe with her class, and was there for her far more than the typical corporate executive is available to his or her children.

Only after this wonderful, family-oriented hiatus did he resume his career and continue his path to the top.

————

I ASPIRED TO go to college because of a man in my community I used to see all the time—he wore a necktie. He was, as a matter of fact, a North Carolina Mutual sales agent by the name of Mr. Marshall Cooper. My dad was always a hard worker, I got that from him. But I went to college because I wanted to be a person like Mr. Cooper who wore a necktie every day.

I have an undergraduate degree in accounting from North Carolina Central University in Durham, North Carolina, and I attained that degree in 1975. After graduation, I worked for two years with PPG Industries in Pittsburgh, Pennsylvania, in the audit department as an internal auditor. After gaining this valuable experience, I returned to school and earned an MBA from Atlanta University in Atlanta, Georgia, now known as Clark Atlanta University.

When I came out of grad school, I had job offers to go into corporate America in an accounting role—one company even made me an offer to become an assistant controller. The corporate offers came with salaries much larger than the offers I had from accounting firms. But the thing I noticed when I was at PPG was that most of the people they were hiring at the higher-level positions were all CPAs and had come from what at the time were the "Big Eight" public accounting firms. So I said to myself, *You have got to get into one of the Big Eight firms because that's what is going to provide you with exceptional business knowledge, training, and growth.*

After receiving offers from all the firms, I went to work for Deloitte & Touche in Raleigh, North Carolina. It was an international accounting firm, and one of the Big Eight. It's now one of the Big Four. Deciding to take that job instead of a corporate one had a tremendous impact on what was to follow.

Now, I say that because everything else I have done in my career has been predicated on the training I got at Deloitte & Touche. If I hadn't gone to work there, I do not think I would have received the training, the foundation, the exposure that has allowed me to do all the things I do today. And since that was very early in my career, it was a significant help to me.

I could only have gotten that very strong accounting background with one of the Big Eight firms. The reason I say that is because I didn't go to a nationally recognized university. I know I got a great education, but when I would tell people I went to North Carolina Central University or that I got my MBA from Atlanta University, most people in the business community in the larger cities outside the South would not have heard of either one.

Later in my career, when I worked at Hardee's as one of their financial executives, I would always get questions about my education and career. I would meet people, and the first thing they would assume was that I was just a division controller, nothing higher. Because I'm African American, they figured I couldn't have a bigger job, I couldn't be a corporate controller. When they found out I *was* the corporate controller, they would always ask, "Where'd you go to school?" Well, I'd give them the answer, but most would not recognize the names.

But then they'd ask, "Where were you before you came to Hardee's?" Then I would say, "I spent twelve years with Deloitte & Touche." Well, that had an effect. All the questions would stop. They knew if I spent twelve years with a firm like Deloitte & Touche, I had to be a top-notch financial person. It gave me instant credibility.

That's why my public accounting background was so

important—with people questioning and thinking, *Well, maybe he's here because they needed an African American for the diversity program.* Deloitte & Touche or one of the other major firms just gave you validation.

Everyone knew that Deloitte & Touche only hired the top students from each graduating class. They wouldn't keep you twelve years—as a matter of fact, they won't keep people past one year—if they thought you didn't have the skills to contribute to the firm.

I spent about nine years with Hardee's. I started as their vice president/controller, three years later was promoted to senior vice president/controller, and after another two and a half years was promoted to senior vice president/chief financial officer and treasurer.

Then, in the year 2000, I decided that I was going to take a break and spend the last two years of my daughter's high school career not working. I wanted to spend time with her, and I was blessed to have done well enough financially to be able to do that. I went to PTA meetings, the ball games, traveled with her class, and had a wonderful time.

The way I got back into the business world and to North Carolina Mutual was through Mr. Bert Collins, who is the current board chairman, and Willie Closs, who was executive vice president of marketing. They approached me about coming to work as a consultant to address some of the accounting issues that were found by their outside auditors—who happened to be Deloitte & Touche.

I had met Willie when we both worked at Deloitte & Touche. And I knew Bert because he was North Carolina Mutual's controller and my client back when I was still with Deloitte & Touche. I managed their outside audits.

When they initially approached me, I said, "I don't want to work anymore, at least not anytime soon." Then about a year and a half or two years later, I agreed to come back as a consultant, basically working one day a week. I never came back to work full-time, and I surely never came back with the intention of becoming president.

However, when I got there, I absolutely loved coming to work! I woke up each day excited. It sounds pretty hokey to think that somebody gets up and is excited about going to work, but that's the way it happened—I was excited about going to North Carolina Mutual.

I kept fighting the feeling, thinking, *You know what? I'm not supposed to enjoy going to work like this. But I'm having fun!* I loved the people there, and I knew a lot of employees from the ten years I spent as an outside auditor. And sometimes I'd even think about old Mr. Marshall Cooper, the North Carolina Mutual insurance agent with the necktie I used to see around the neighborhood when I was a kid.

## JOSEPH PLUMERI
**Chairman and CEO, Willis Group Holdings Ltd.**

Joseph Plumeri would probably agree that his entire career, successful and distinguished as it has been, began as the result of dumb luck—he found himself in the wrong place at the right time.

Plumeri's accidental start in business developed into a lifelong career in banking and insurance, where he rose to the highest positions in his profession: president of Smith Barney Shearson, president of Shearson Lehman Brothers, CEO and chairman of Travelers Primerica Financial Services, and CEO of Citibank North America. Now chairman and CEO of the global firm Willis Group Holdings Ltd., the world's third-largest insurance broker with more than 400 offices in nearly 120 countries, Plumeri enjoys the distinction of being the first non-British chairman in the company's history. Plumeri is a second-generation Italian American. His grandparents came from Sicily. He says his arrival at the ultra-proper Willis Group was "sort of like Fonzie showing up."

Fonzie or not, Plumeri has done a spectacular job at Willis: before he joined up, the company had been purchased by the leveraged buyout firm KKR for $3 a share. With Plumeri at the helm, the stock climbed as high as $46.50. By all accounts, it is a great success story. In the last seven years, Willis went from making no money at all to becoming the best-performing company in its sector with the highest margins of any global insurance broker.

Perhaps there really are no accidents.

―――――

IN 1968 I registered for my first year of classes at New York Law School. When I found out that my classes would be over at noon every day, I decided to go out and find an afternoon job with a law firm. That way, in the morning I would learn the law academically and in the afternoon I would learn it practically.

So I walked around New York City and looked at lobby directories and buildings that had three names on them—because I thought that if a firm had three names it had to be a law firm. What the hell did I know?

Somewhere on Broad Street I saw the names "Carter, Berlind and Weill." I assumed it was a law firm because . . . well . . . it had three names. So I went up the elevator, and I said to the receptionist, "Who can I see about a job?"

She made a call and said, "Go down to the hall and make a left and ask for Mr. Weill."

I walked into the office, and Mr. Weill said, "What can I do for you?"

I replied, "Well, I'd really like to learn the law. I'm taking classes in the morning and learning what the law school has to teach me, and in the afternoon I'd really like to work at a law firm and learn the practical aspects of the law." I mean, I made a really terrific speech—it was great.

Mr. Weill said, "That's a great idea. What makes you think you'll learn the law here?"

I answered, "Well, it's a law firm."

He responded, "No, this is not a law firm. This is a brokerage firm."

In those days there were millions of little securities firms all over the city, and this was one of them. Obviously I was in the wrong spot. I was a little disconcerted . . . I remember I was sitting in a leather chair, and I kind of slid down it because I was so embarrassed. But then I got up and started to walk out, and he spoke up, "No, no, this is interesting."

Long story short, he gave me an afternoon after-school job. I remember my office was a closet—literally. They took a door off and stuck a desk in a closet. Half the desk was in and half was sticking out in the hallway. People would walk by, call me "Joey Baby," and hit me in the back of the head.

Mr. Weill, you may have guessed, turned out to be Sandy Weill, who built the brokerage, banking, and insurance empire that eventually became Citigroup, with Sandy as chairman and CEO.

Carter, Berlind and Weill grew to be Shearson Lehman Brothers, which merged into Smith Barney, and so on. I rose as the company grew—up from the closet, so to speak. So my pivotal moment professionally came while I was looking for a law job, accidentally walked into Mr. Weill's brokerage firm, met Sandy, and took that part-time job.

It was a total accident. By just getting off my ass—excuse the expression—and knocking on doors, I made something happen. When I give commencement speeches or motivational speeches and I give the audience my list of things that you've got to do in life, number one is "go play in traffic." Just go do something. You never know what will happen. Look what happened to me.

I grew along with all of Sandy's mergers and acquisitions—all the way to Citigroup. I was at Citigroup and all the earlier Weill-led companies for thirty-two years, which I guess is astounding in itself these days. I did everything from go out for doughnuts and deliver people's laundry when I started. I rose to be president of Smith Barney Shearson. I was CEO of Primerica Financial Services, and I was CEO of Citibank North America, and a lot of things in between.

At Citibank I oversaw its 450 retail branches, and with Travelers Primerica Financial Services we had 150,000 personal financial analysts with about 6 million clients.

What a great mistake I made that day.

## CLARENCE C. BARKSDALE
### Chairman and CEO, Centerre Bancorporation

We all know about "lifers"—people who spent their entire career at the same company because they got comfortable in a job, burrowed in, and rode out a predictable career. Clarence "Cedge" Barksdale is a different kind of lifer: although he spent his entire professional life at the same company, he became a dynamic, successful leader whose career was far from scripted.

In the course of that career, Barksdale built the First National Bank in St. Louis into one of the powerhouse financial institutions in the Midwest. Pushing for organic growth as well as growth through acquisitions, he transformed the sleepy firm into a $7 billion banking center that became known as Centerre Bancorporation. After several mergers and acquisitions, the company is now part of Bank of America.

Barksdale's defining decision was a decision to stay put—to remain at the St. Louis bank despite an attractive offer and some eager recruiting by a bigger bank in another city. His decision, which was driven partly by family and partly by career and business, was nevertheless 100 percent savvy. In fact, the two driving factors merged to create a powerful winning combination for the bank, for its employees and customers, and for Barksdale himself.

————————

DURING THE KOREAN War, I volunteered to serve with the Counter Intelligence Corps of the Army, where I learned the fine art of espionage. I was stationed in Berlin for two and a half years, and when I came back I started at Washington University Law School. This was in 1957. One night I went to a party and met the woman who would become my wife—her name is Nini. I think I instantly fell in love with her. With that, and the fact that I was not really enjoying law school, I told Dad I was going to quit. He said, "Why don't you just come and work at the law firm for the summer (my father was a prominent attorney) and see if you enjoy working in the law."

So I went to his firm for the summer, and they sent me to work in the library, which was where they started young lawyers in training. This was not where I wanted to be. After the summer was over, Dad said, "Well, how do you feel about the law, Cedge?"

I replied, "I'm not going back to law school. I'm going to get a job, and I may ask Nini to marry me."

I didn't contemplate living anywhere other than St. Louis, so I went downtown and interviewed for a number of jobs. I received several offers, and one was from the First National Bank in St. Louis. I visited the bank and looked around and saw mostly older people working there. I presumed that a job there would turn out to be a great opportunity, especially if they were to place me in the management training program. That's what they did, and I remained at the bank my entire career.

When I was still very young and working at First National, I was offered a job in Cleveland at the old Cleveland Trust Company, which was a bigger bank than we were. It was quite an experience for me personally—being wooed by them. The bank's board asked me there for dinner, and it was quite a rush. But Nini and I decided we didn't really want to make the move to Cleveland.

Looking back, that decision was a crucial point in my career as far as my personal ambitions were concerned. I decided not to move, but instead to stay where I was. I knew that First National had a lot of potential, and I was determined to really build it up. I ended up doing that with the help of a great many good people.

Nini really influenced my decision to stay. Her entire family lived in St. Louis and had been there for generations. It was important to her to stay. I think the decision really pleased her, and she ended up being a great help in building the bank. She would go to conventions and help out in many different ways.

She was the best salesperson we had in the company. When I took her to conventions, she would get all the wives to help out and give receptions. People loved that. They really enjoyed coming to our parties because our wives were more experienced with entertaining than we were—much better at socializing than we were. And Nini set the example for us.

When I was made president of the bank, the chairman slapped me on the back and said, "Cedge, I'm gonna tell you right now, the only reason you're being named president of the bank at such a young age is because of Nini."

I grew up in the bank as a commercial lender, and we really built the bank on my efforts in that area. I worked in what we called "new business." I traveled a lot. When I started out, my first territory was Philadelphia, then Buffalo, and eventually New York City. This part of the job, I think, is the reason I was so successful: I was the biggest "business getter" by far in the bank. At some point the chairman said he thought that in two years' time I'd brought in more business than any one person had *ever* brought into the bank.

At the time of the Cleveland offer, I was already executive vice president at First National, and I was fairly certain I was going to be named president in the near future. And in fact I attained the position of president at the age of thirty-seven.

When I became president of the bank, I continued being involved in the sales end. I always said that the president and leader of any organization should be its best salesman. I advise young people to develop their sales skills because they'll need them throughout their careers, no matter how much they achieve. By its very title, the president should be its best salesman. Customers are very flattered when the president calls on them.

When I took charge of the bank, we became very aggressive. I had a great many ideas about growing our corporate business, and we developed a fine reputation here in the center of the country. We did what we called "cash management"—speeding up the collection of your receipts—and we really expanded that activity.

Eventually we decided to go after international business. At first, I tried to cover the entire world in one year, from Asia to Europe to South America. When it was over, I said, "I can't do this anymore." We worked up a very simple coverage plan among three people: our executive VP, Dick Ford; our chairman, Ted Jones; and myself. I said, "Look, we'll divide up the world. I'll take South America, and you guys decide where you want to go. Ted, where do you want to go?"

Ted said, "I want to go to Asia."

Dick said, "I'll go to Europe."

That's what transpired. The three of us became a sales team— the top three officers in the bank. We really built up the bank in that way.

With our new, grander strategy, we also decided to change the name to Centerre Bancorp, a much more dynamic name that was big in scope and had no limitations. It had a strong impact and showed we were not simply a local bank anymore—that we had national and international objectives. Our growth greatly accelerated after the name change—not because of it, but it did represent our change in attitude, effort, and mission.

Our growth was always outside of the main bank because we sold ourselves all over the world. Eventually, we started to buy other banks. When you buy a $10 million bank—say, down in Branson, Missouri—you'll get $10 million in loans and deposits overnight. The acquisition didn't cost us anything except for hotel and airplane tickets!

So I spent my entire business career with the same bank. When I started with First National, it had about $500 million in assets, and when I retired at age fifty-six, it was a $7 billion bank. With my original decision to remain at First National, it certainly wasn't a decision to stay still—just a recognition that we could make good things happen from the foundation we already had if we did it right!

## GERALD GREENWALD
### Chairman and CEO, United Airlines; Vice Chairman, Chrysler Corporation

Talk about déjà vu: as of this writing, the state of the American automobile industry seems exceedingly familiar, a replay, in fact, of 1979. That was the year when the Chrysler Corporation came very close to going under and was saved only by what at the time were unprecedented loan guarantees provided by the federal government.

buy furniture to scale

* make it multi functional

add color w/ accents

the Match game

Gerald Greenwald played a major role in securing those loan guarantees and in nursing the auto company back to health.

Greenwald was in place and able to take on these tasks because he had decided to accept legendary auto executive Lee Iacocca's offer to join him at Chrysler. I think readers will find the circumstances leading up to that moment both amusing and instructive as a lesson in the right and wrong ways to approach an important job offer.

The two years after the guarantees were granted turned out to be the most exciting and memorable of Greenwald's career as he and his team, under Lee Iacocca, brought Chrysler back to life.

His story reverberates with relevant echoes of the past and the present. His take on Henry Ford II explains a great deal about why Detroit is in its current fix. His take on the inner workings of Washington is insightful and memorable. He told me, for example, that he learned from former House majority leader Thomas P. "Tip" O'Neill that, in Washington, "you can be dead right, and still be dead."

His observations on the entire 1979 auto meltdown and recovery are fascinating in light of the problems facing the auto industry today.

————

I WAS WITH Ford Motor Company for twenty-two years, three different times outside of the United States working at or directing subsidiaries. I worked in the United Kingdom, France, Brazil, Argentina, and Venezuela; I ran Ford Venezuela.

It was a wonderful time for me. It was a time when American industry was breaking out all over the world, and we were strong, and we knew what we were doing. But in retrospect, we didn't have enough competition pushing back at us. While it was a wonderful time, I guess, like many mature industries and companies, it went soft.

At the time, Henry Ford II was running Ford. He was like a well-meaning emperor. "Well-meaning" in the sense that I don't think he ever realized that he acted like one. And all the people at Ford Motor Company and those who worked for him outside of Ford Motor Company certainly treated him like one.

A friend of mine, Hal Sperlich, got fired because he pressed Henry Ford too hard to build small cars. He wanted to build a small car to compete with the Japanese, who were just beginning to make inroads in California. Henry Ford made a famous statement: "Small cars, small profits—bullshit!"

If someone had an idea, they had to make Ford think it was his idea or they had a problem. If anyone in the company tried to compete with Henry, he'd fire him. That was the worst of Henry Ford. The best of him was that he really cared about his company. He worked hard. I got him to stand in a receiving line in Venezuela to shake dealers' hands for two hours. I never saw any of the bad side, but I would hear about it.

I was doing well. I loved what I was doing at Ford. When I arrived in Venezuela to run the subsidiary there, I discovered that the Venezuelan government, flush with oil revenue, had decided they were smart enough to pass some decrees that would change the auto industry to make it more to their liking. I read all this and thought, *If these rules are implemented, the whole industry will be destroyed, and so, one way or another, they won't be implemented.* I turned out to be right. And so, while my competitors stood still waiting for these new rules to happen, I didn't wait around for any changes that might restrict us. I ran the business as it should have been run, without worrying about what the government might or might not do. And it was a great run. Employment at the company tripled, profits were up tenfold, and our market share doubled.

So there I was. Then one day I got a message to call Lee Iacocca. He had been running Ford and had made the company tremendously successful. But in the process he clashed with Henry Ford. Ford fired him, and Iacocca went off to run Chrysler. He started at Chrysler just six weeks before his call to me. I assumed that he was calling to get my thoughts on Chrysler's Latin American business. But Glenda, my wife, looked at the message and simply said, "Don't call him back." Somehow she knew what Iacocca was up to.

Iacocca wanted to talk to me about coming to Chrysler to work with him as the company's controller. My response to him was, "I don't want to be a financial guy anymore. I'd love to run a company or a subsidiary." He promised that after a year or two he'd put me in to run the truck division. But as it turned out, that never happened.

I called friends all over the world to get their advice about taking the job. Finally, my wife said, "What are you doing?" And I said, "Well, I'm trying to get some—"

"Wait a minute," she said. "You're going to keep calling people until somebody says, 'Why *don't* you take the job?'" She knew I wanted to go. I looked at her and said, "I think you're right." And I went.

I went because I was thinking of the situation this way: working here at a small Ford subsidiary, I'm like a pitcher in the minors, and a major league team calls and says, "Look, we've got some problems up here and need your help. Would you like to pitch for us in the World Series?"

That's exactly what it felt like when I arrived at Chrysler—like I went from the minor leagues to playing in the World Series in an instant.

By the way, when I left for Chrysler, Henry Ford was the only one who understood what I was up to. He said, "You're in it for the challenge, and bless you for it."

Looking at it another way, the Chrysler job was a huge opportunity and a challenge to go to a company that was in real trouble, where I could make a difference.

This was in 1979. I went to Chrysler as vice president and

controller. And after working there for three weeks, I had to admit, "Man, this is the dumbest thing I've ever done."

I hadn't really done a full analytical due diligence before accepting Iacocca's offer. Good thing I didn't. What I found there was such a mess that, had I known, I would have been scared off. I never would have gone—and never had the great experiences I ended up having.

Chrysler was in terrible shape. It was awful. It was being run by "financial engineers." These were people who did not understand the guts of the business—operations, distribution, dealerships, product. They knew how to manipulate financials, but they didn't know how to run a car business, and they were ruining it.

With Chrysler in real trouble and in danger of failing, I ended up negotiating the now-famous government loan guarantees that gave the company a breather and helped save it.

It was a great experience—I learned a lot about Washington. I saw democracy in its purest at work. And it was beautiful, it really was. The case we were making was that the country was in or near a recession and an enormous number of jobs would be lost if Chrysler went down. We did computer runs of the number of employees that Chrysler, our suppliers, and our dealers had in each congressman's district and made the case that they had to vote for the loan guarantees in order to save those jobs. The total number was 500,000.

The House vote was easy. Now the Senate—I'll never forget that.

Senators from places like Utah and the Dakotas would say, "Tell me again why I ought to risk my constituents' tax dollars by giving guarantees, when the average wage in my state is seven dollars an hour, and these guarantees are protecting twenty-dollar-an-hour jobs? What's this about?"

And so we had to really work hard on the Senate side, and until the last day we were not at all certain it would pass. I learned that congressional committees will try to defer controversial decisions if they can. To this day I don't know why I had the courage to do this, but during Iacocca's testimony in December 1979 they said they wanted to postpone the vote to February when they reconvened. I asked to make a statement and in so many words said, "You've already decided. If you postpone to February, we'll be gone. Chrysler will be dead."

Of course, that statement hit the press, and back in Detroit they were saying, "Are you crazy, announcing our death like that?" But in the matter of a week the Congress came around. And so now it's near Christmas, and the House and Senate are both getting ready to vote.

But then we faced a filibuster in the Senate. Senator Tom Eagleton comes out of the Senate chamber with his shirttail hanging out and says, basically, "Here's what's going to happen, and you've got to tell me if you want to do this or not: you tell me what you want on the guarantees. I'll convene a caucus of the key guys from both parties. Then I'll come back out and I'll tell you what you can have. And you'll have to decide whether you want it—you'll have to say yes or no. If you say yes, then it will get approved by the Senate. If you say no, it's over."

And I said, "Okay, what the hell else am I going to do?" He comes rushing back out five hours later and says, "Here's the deal: you get everything but the interim financing."

"Translation," I said. "We can only live for two months, and you want us to renegotiate all four hundred of our loans, get new loans from five states, get the Canadians to agree to loan guarantees, and renegotiate terms with our suppliers and our unions. We're going to do all that, but we can't get that done in two months."

"Well, I'm sorry, but you can't have interim financing because these senators believe that once you have interim financing you'll have the government hooked and you'll manipulate and you won't comply with all the things that you need to do."

And I said, "Well, that's silly."

He said, "Remember? Yes or no?"

So I said, "Well, if I say no, we die; if I say yes, it's a long shot, but we can try." So I said yes. The loan guarantees were approved, and early in January, at the end of Jimmy Carter's term, he signed the law in a White House ceremony that we attended. He signed with two pens, and he handed out fifty.

That was just the beginning. When guys talk about being in the zone, it's usually a sport. But I had that experience at Chrysler for the next two years—I worked, I slept little, and I ate little. I was always on the run—every day for two years. Every morning I'd wake up and I'd think, *I don't know what it's going to be, but there will be at least one, maybe two life-threatening events for Chrysler today. But I'll solve them—not me alone, but me and my guys will solve them.* And off we'd go, and sure enough, the events came.

And here's my main point: I was in some kind of zone. In those two years I never got sick. I didn't catch a cold. I didn't have the flu. I didn't feel tired. But as soon as the crisis started to ease, I started getting sick. In fact, I was sick for six months. So I was in that zone for two years. And those two years became the most rewarding experience in my life.

# CHAPTER 2

# Leaving the Mother Ship: Taking the Entrepreneurial Leap

Who sits atop the pyramid of American business? Which executives garner the most respect and admiration? Is it the captains of industry—the Wall Street titans, the real estate moguls, the oil barons? Don't those labels sound a little nefarious? But say the word "entrepreneur" and nothing less than the American Dream comes to mind.

Entrepreneurs are the romantic heroes of the business world. They are our modern-day explorers and pioneers. They take an idea from scratch, strike out on their own, and risk it all. You can almost hear Sinatra singing "My Way" in the background as these rugged individualists spread their business plans over kitchen tables late at night.

I've worked with entrepreneurs, lifelong "company men," family-run company owners, public-company executives, Wall Street financiers, lawyers, accountants, and more. I don't think there is much dispute: entrepreneurs are wired a little differently. They aren't any smarter or more capable—they're just on a different kind of quest.

Imagine leaving a company where you are at the top or rising to it, like the executives in this chapter, and deciding that you need something more. Not pay or perks, but something intangible that's missing in the corporate environment.

More often than not, that intangible is *control*. Control over one's life and the direction of one's business. Of course, people also take the entrepreneurial leap with the dream of becoming wildly successful, but among the entrepreneurs I've known, and in my own experience, it is not the dream of great wealth as much as the desire to direct one's own destiny that drives the entrepreneur.

For many entrepreneurs, taking the leap is, as Danny Meyer said in the previous chapter, an itch that must be scratched. That's what the executives in this chapter felt, and it was the same with me. I led a group to buy back our family-owned drugstore chain from Pet, Inc., because I wanted to regain control, not so much of the asset itself but of my life, career, and professional destiny. As I saw decisions being made that had an impact on me, or decisions being made that I disagreed with, I soon realized that I would not be happy unless I was at the helm. If there were mistakes to be made, I wanted them to be my mistakes. If there were calculated risks to be taken, I wanted them to be my calculations.

So when is the right time to take the entrepreneurial leap? Everyone says to the would-be entrepreneur, "Go for it. Chase your dream." Of course they say that—it's ingrained in our DNA to support pioneers and explorers, and nobody wants to get in the way of someone else's dream. But unless your advisers are jumping off the cliff with you, that advice should be taken with a big grain of salt. If people are being honest with you, you're going to get opinions on both sides. That's because there is no such thing as a sure thing. A great business concept carried out with poor management and execution will fail. Not all businesses have the bones to be successful, but of those that do, it is still easier to fail than to succeed. When professional investors look at a business plan, they do it coldly. And that's the way entrepreneurs should look at their plans too . . . that is, if they possess the ability to critically self-assess.

Too often, entrepreneurs fall hopelessly in love with their ideas and lose their objectivity. The phrase "love is blind" is even more true in start-ups. Ask a young entrepreneur looking for funding in Silicon Valley who his competitors are, and more often than not he'll say something like, "Our [fill-in-the-blank product, service, market niche, or technology] is so unique in the marketplace that we really don't have head-on competition." What's that again? A company with no competition? Ask the successful, battle-tested entrepreneurs about their experiences, and you'll often hear, "If I had known then what I know now about our business, I never would have tried this." And that's from the successful ones.

Of course, entrepreneurs have to have a little swagger—or a lot of it—and maybe a little naïveté at the outset is a good thing too, but that doesn't mean they can throw common sense out the window. A commitment to creating a bold new company based on a new set of rules doesn't give entrepreneurs permission to make up their own economic reality. When entrepreneurs go around with their business plans, they love to show the "hockey stick" revenue growth plan (slower growth in the first phase while the product builds its market, followed by much steeper growth as the product takes over). But just because a PowerPoint slide says it will happen doesn't make it so, and entrepreneurs have to be careful not to start drinking their own Kool-Aid. Being realistic about the company's market, competitive advantage, weaknesses, and financial projections doesn't just prevent some big mistakes—it also allows the entrepreneur and business team to properly plan the company's strategy and use of capital.

Perhaps the hardest thing for any would-be entrepreneur to evaluate is whether he or she really would be a good chief executive. Of course, everyone likes to think they can be a great leader, but a lot of people are great number-twos, not great number-ones.

It can be lonely at the top. When things go well, it's a tremendous place to be, but when challenges arise—and they always do—the chief executive has got to have the shoulders to bear the weight. It's not for everyone. A lot of business leaders thrive on being the one who calls the shots, and it takes a certain confidence (and maybe a touch of arrogance at times) to pull it off.

One asset I've found indispensable is a confidant outside the company—someone who can be trusted and who can serve as a sounding board when needed. Sometimes you need that outside perspective from someone at a distance from the situation, someone who can see things from a fresh vantage point. It may be a friend, a peer in another company, a mentor from the past, or even an executive coach. I was lucky. I married my lifelong confidant. She was my sounding board and my rock when I needed it. She didn't always see it my way—which means she was doing her job—but she always had one and only one agenda: my best interest.

What I love about this chapter is that the people here exemplify the best qualities of the entrepreneur. Whether starting a real estate company in Vermont, a dot-com in Silicon Valley, or a renewable energy firm in Atlanta, would-be entrepreneurs find important lessons and inspiration for the hard work ahead. The highly successful businesspeople in this chapter knew what they were doing. They were realistic about their prospects, they worked their tails off, and—cue Sinatra—they did it their way.

# BILL RASMUSSEN
**Founder and CEO, ESPN**

---

Bill Rasmussen exhibited the entrepreneurial spark as a young man just out of the U.S. Air Force. Working briefly in the advertising department of Westinghouse, he saw an opportunity to provide better work and greater value for the company as an outside contractor. He promptly quit, set up a company, and secured Westinghouse as his first customer.

Bill became the consummate entrepreneur—a visionary with unlimited energy and passion. Throughout his career he has shown that he can conceptualize a new and exciting business idea and then bring it to life successfully.

Bill is willing to break the rules and push the boundaries, as he did when he started ESPN, the twenty-four-hour cable sports network. There were times when he didn't quite know how to get to the next step in his quest to start a cable sports network, but his guts, his brilliance, and his willingness to take risks got him through and on to the next step. Eventually he figured things out and made history.

When Bill Rasmussen is around, there is electricity and drama in the air. You know he is someone special, and investors and customers know it too. He was able to bring in large, sophisticated companies as investors, sponsors, and advertisers—including Getty Oil and Anheuser-Busch—for the fledgling network.

Bill's risks paid off for himself, his investors, and legions of sports fans. He elevated sports news coverage to a new and sophisticated level, and he brought thousands of sporting events— some heretofore obscure ones—front and center in the American consciousness. He put cable sports on the map.

Bill and his investors sold ESPN in 1984 to the ABC television network for $237.5 million. At the time, Bill and his family owned

12.32 percent of the company. He could have hung on longer and made even more money in the business, but he chose not to.

People ask Bill, "Don't you feel bad that you got out so soon?" And he tells them, "No, I've lived an amazing life since 1984, and I have found total fulfillment."

———

To UNDERSTAND THE defining moment in my career, we have to go back to the time I got fired from my job as communications director with the Hartford Whalers hockey team.

It was Memorial Day 1978. I was about to go play golf, and I got the call: "You're done. You're not coming back to work."

The decision was no surprise, since I had had disagreements with management about a variety of things during my four years with the team. My son Scott worked for them as well, and he was fired too. Well, that's the way it goes. I didn't play golf very well that day because the call was kind of disrupting.

The following Tuesday I had been scheduled to tape a TV show about the Whalers. I called Ed Eagen. Ed was an independent producer trying to break into cable TV with sports packages. Ed was one of the original investors in ESPN. I said to Ed, "You don't want to talk to me. I'm not really high on the Whalers at the moment."

He said, "Well, come on in, and we'll talk anyway." And so we talked about what we could do together—just a rambling conversation—and he said, "We ought to do something in sports, hockey. . . ."

Before the month of June had passed, Scott, Ed, and I called a press conference and said we were going to set up a cable network to show Connecticut sports teams. We'd do University of Connecticut sports and Wesleyan University and the New Haven teams and a whole bunch more—all of the schools in Connecticut, really. We were going to show basketball and then expand it to add football and all the sports, including college baseball and the college World Series.

We needed a way to get these games into the cable systems and thought the best way was to do it via satellite. We found out we could rent a satellite transponder from RCA Americom. They had launched a satellite in December 1976. The transponders are the relay devices in the satellite. They receive the signal aimed at the satellite from Earth, and they turn the signal around and send it back down to everywhere in North America. It is a single pulse going up and an "umbrella" when it comes back down. And when it comes down, it gets fed into the cable systems and then into viewers' homes via the cable.

The cable people suggested I call RCA about a transponder, but I'm thinking: *Here I am, a little guy from the South Side of Chicago, I just got fired, and I'm going to call RCA in New York and they're going to even pick up the phone?*

I called and the response was, "Where are you in Connecticut? I'll be up there tomorrow morning." I didn't know at the time, but they couldn't give the transponders away. So, sure, they were interested in talking to me.

The salesman came up and explained how everything worked and the rates for the transponder: $1,250 for five hours at night. Then he said, "We have this other rate that no one's ever called on, so we don't have it on our rate sheet. It's twenty-four hours a day, seven days a week, for five years—$34,167 a month."

My son Scott, who is very quick with numbers, jumped in and said, "That can't be right. That would come to only $1,143 for the whole twenty-four-hour day, versus $1,250 for just five hours a night!"

The salesman replied, "That's what it says here." And he showed us the tariff.

He left and we're talking this over, and I said to Scott, "You know, we ought to lock in that thing." So we called the RCA salesman the next morning and said, "We'll take one of those things." We didn't even know what to call it.

The salesman said, "One of what things?"

"One of those twenty-four-hour things you were describing yesterday."

The salesman said, "You will?"

And so we had our transponder, and we had our satellite feed . . . but we didn't know what to do with it. We had the ability to run programming twenty-four hours a day, and that was where we got the idea to put on a twenty-four-hour network—but the only problem was that we didn't have the programming to pull it off.

Well, at least the financial arrangements were in our favor, and it gave us time to figure things out. We were able to commit to the deal with no money down. And the way it worked was that RCA would wait to bill us ninety days after our first usage of the transponder, and then they'd give us another thirty days to pay. That's a pretty good deal by any measure.

We incorporated on June 14, 1978, and the breakthrough idea for ESPN came on August 16, 1978. The reason I know it so well is it's my daughter's birthday. We were in a traffic jam in Connecticut on Route 84 going down to New Jersey to celebrate with her.

At that point we already had the transponder, and Scott and I were trying to determine what our programming would consist of. It's a tough question, because you get a lot of programming, but you chew it up in a half hour and boom, what do you put on next?

We were talking and throwing around ideas, and Scott was taking notes on a yellow pad. We came up with the idea of going to the NCAA, since they conducted over 116,000 sanctioned events each year. An arrangement with them would solve our programming need. We wouldn't be able to televise football right away, because the NCAA was under contract with the networks, but we could tape-delay football games for replay at 10:30 PM each night. However, we would have access to live basketball and countless other sports events.

Being a sportscaster, I was always frustrated about having only about three minutes to report on sports. I was telling this to Scott, and then I came up with another idea: "You know what we should do? We should have a half-hour sports show."

Scott liked the idea. "We can fill up the show with all kinds of game highlights."

And then I said, "You know what we're going to do? We're going to put it on at six-thirty in the evening opposite the ABC, NBC, and CBS evening news broadcasts."

When I took that idea to the cable industry, everyone said, "That's suicide. Nobody is ever going to watch it. Everybody watches the evening news."

Back in those days everybody did. At that time, 93 percent of viewership in America was among ABC, CBS, and NBC.

Well, guess what? Not everybody wants to watch the evening news. When we put *SportsCenter* on, people began to discover it. People who had been watching the 6:30 news started moving to our sports news.

Putting *SportsCenter* on opposite the evening news of ABC, CBS, and NBC at 6:30 PM Eastern Time was the single most important decision I ever made. It was certainly my defining moment. The decision to do a half-hour sports show and run it opposite the network news put us on the map.

The idea was new and important because up until then the news programs only gave sports a couple of minutes—just a few reports on scores and such. So this made a huge statement by giving sports news the kind of in-depth coverage it had never enjoyed on television before. It was the greatest sports show ever. It still is today. It was the only consistent program we ever had. It caught on, and viewers started switching from CBS, NBC, and ABC news.

I think it really made ESPN what it is today. And you know, we did it almost by accident. When I came up with the idea, we were just stretching our imaginations as we considered what kind of programming we could put on.

ESPN went on the air September 7, 1979. It sounds funny now, but our first programs were Irish hurling, Australian rules football, and kickboxing. On September 1, 1980, we went full-time with full programming twenty-four hours a day.

I took a lot of chances and a lot of risk to get ESPN up and running. One day I looked at my bank book and I had $17.28 in my account, but I was determined to keep going. I didn't know where the rest of it was coming from, but I didn't let that stop me.

My total investment was $9,000 from a cash advance on my credit card. My father, mother, sister, and brother put in some money also. Plus, we found a small investment banking firm in Pennsylvania that eventually came up with about $275,000. They took us around to potential investors and served as our investment banker. They were able to get us connected with Getty Oil, who originally invested $20 million and had invested $146 million before ESPN turned the corner. Getty owned 85 percent of the company, and we owned the rest.

Our first big sponsor was Anheuser-Busch. It was the biggest single contract, at that point, ever spent in cable. In our own infinite wisdom, once we got the idea that we were going to do this big network, we decided that we would get eight sponsors at $2,760,000 each. I don't remember where we came up with this funny number, it was just a number.

We said, "Budweiser is the biggest sports advertiser. Let's go to New York and talk to their agency." By that time we felt we could talk to anybody. That was in January 1979, still some nine months from going on the air. We went down to New York and met the vice president of advertising at D'Arcy McManus, the advertising agency for Anheuser-Busch. We told him that for $2,760,000 Budweiser would have the exclusive in the beer category. He looked at us like we were from the planet Mars and said, "Hum, I don't know. We'll have to talk about all this."

Looking right over his shoulder out of the window, I could see the side of a New York building with a big Miller Beer sign. I said, "Well, there are a lot of other opportunities out there for us." He asked us if we could come back tomorrow, so that he could think about our conversation.

We went back the next day, and he said he had talked to the brewery. "We'll give you $500,000." Now, I'm still working off my credit card, but I worked up the guts to say, "No, we are going to continue our discussions elsewhere."

Well, he blinked.

By the time we got back to Connecticut—we were working from there at the time—he was on the phone and said, "Can you come back tomorrow morning?" So back we went the next day. This time he said, "We'll give you $1,380,000, half your package price. Will that get us in the game?"

This became our first advertising contract, and Anheuser-Busch became our first advertiser. The $1,380,000 price tag was the biggest to date in cable.

While I was setting things up and taking all these crazy risks, I didn't even think about the negatives. I always knew it was going to work. Suppose Getty had said no when we approached them? Getty was the eighth company that we went to for sponsorship, as the first seven said no. But we just kept on going. And if Getty had said no, we'd have a ninth one to talk to, and we would have kept going until one of them said, "Yes!"

# DAVID L. STEWARD
**Founder, Chairman, and CEO, World Wide Technology**

D avid Steward has always been driven by two forces: faith in God and scripture, and innovative, out-of-the-box thinking. In spite of growing up poor, and in spite of his early struggles in school—he was a C student and had to work hard for those Cs—those two forces propelled him to great heights in the high-tech field and gave him a sense of accomplishment that only he could create for himself.

World Wide Technology, the company Steward founded, is the largest African American–owned business in the United States, with sales of over $2.5 billion annually. Steward is also the author of *Doing Business by the Good Book: 52 Lessons on Success Straight from the Bible*.

The seeds of Steward's entrepreneurship were planted at a very early age. As a youngster, he worked at various jobs to have some money in his pocket. As an adult, the entrepreneurial phase of his career began when he founded a company that discovered and recovered overcharges in the bills that railroads and other carriers sent to his clients.

The concept was new, and the company's mission reflected Steward's innovative bent along with his desire to serve, which developed from his religious faith. He began to pioneer the use of emerging computer and database technologies in his work and discovered new ways to benefit his business clients. This ultimately turned into his next company, and his innovative approaches propelled the spectacular growth and success of World Wide Technology.

Success in the corporate world came early for Steward, well before he became an entrepreneur. As a young man working for Federal Express, he found creative and innovative ways to serve his clients, and his grateful company acknowledged and rewarded his work. His future looked bright—but success, like beauty, is in the eye of the beholder. The more he achieved at FedEx, the more he felt there was something else out there for him, something bigger for him to do. His faith and his drive allowed him to take a big step away from the secure and well-trodden path of corporate life into an unknowable but exciting entrepreneurial future.

————

I WAS ALWAYS an entrepreneur—hustling or doing something. I call it hustling, but in a good way. I was always a pretty good sales guy, and when I was ten or eleven years old, I was selling Christmas cards door to door so I could have money to buy presents for all my siblings and my mother and father. That was my first real entrepreneurial experience, and that's what I think led me into business, or at least wanting to learn about business. And that's why I majored in business in school.

After school and a number of different jobs, I went to work for Federal Express in 1978 and stayed for six years. It was a tremendous experience because I was in sales and had the opportunity to look closely at a great variety of businesses, see how they were run and how you can bring value to them by solving their problems. I think the experience of selling to corporate customers and knowing how to build relationships based on integrity and a core set of values certainly helped me in everything I've done.

FedEx was also a great experience because the company was enterprising, entrepreneurial, creative, and open to new ideas. It was a company that had a lot of energy and passion. People there were excited about being innovative and saw themselves as explorers in the air express industry. To be in an environment that encouraged innovation, to have access to the company's leaders, and to see how the company was willing to change in order to perfect themselves as they developed the industry—well, it was a good, solid learning experience. When I started, FedEx was shipping maybe ten thousand packages a day. When I left, they were doing maybe a quarter of a million.

The turning point in my career came when I was named salesman of the year . . . but this turning point came not for the reason you might think. I had always been pretty creative in my approach to clients and, in particular, in finding out-of-the-box solutions that solved their business needs. One year I had done a couple of interesting things, went well over my sales goal, and did some innovative work with major clients. FedEx recognized me for what I had done by giving me an award.

At our annual sales event, there was an awards dinner, and they called my name. I came out in front of all these people—eight or nine hundred people. Fred Smith was there. They handed me this inscribed silver ice bucket and took me aside to take pictures. Then it happened. I looked in the bucket, this nice, shiny, new bucket. I looked down to the bottom, and all I could think was, all I could see was, that it was *empty*.

It was an epiphany—call it a revelation. The ice bucket was empty. It made me realize that something was missing. Yes, I accomplished a lot for this great company, and yes, they're recognizing me. You don't know how much I appreciated that. But at that moment I was overcome by the feeling that I had much more to do. And I wasn't going to do it there—I needed to do it on my own. The recognition and the achievements gave me the confidence I needed. I sat down then and said to myself that if I could do all this in a large-company environment, I could do it out in the wider world and have my own, even greater, success.

The fact that these eight hundred people recognized and appreciated that I had done something special—that took me over the top. And then looking in that empty bucket . . . it all came together at that moment. I was able to look beyond my current circumstances. I had a wife who believed in me, but I didn't have any money. I had two children, and a mortgage like everybody else. If I fell off the trapeze, there was no net down there to catch me.

But what I had was faith and eventually a vision and a strategy. In time, I was able to surround myself with great, smart people, and we made it happen. But at that time the question was: How was I going to find this opportunity? How was I going to create it? I began to learn that if you have faith, all things are possible.

There's a favorite scripture of mine that says, "It's impossible to please God without faith." And scripture teaches us that "all is possible with a good measure of faith," and in Hebrews: "Faith is the substance of things hoped for, the evidence of things unseen." I believe in something beyond my circumstances, a belief in the unseen.

Of course, I had doubters and those who wanted to stop me from making a mistake. From family and friends and colleagues, I heard it all: "I want to protect you, so I've got to warn you—you're jumping outside of the box." "Why are you doing this? You're a smart guy. You went to college. You've got a great job. Don't throw that away." "In twenty-five, thirty, forty years, you can get a gold watch and can retire with some decent money."

I knew that I didn't accept this kind of brainwashing—the idea that you have to live in the box in order to have some level of success. And more importantly, I knew that faith without corresponding works is dead, so I acted on my faith and went out on my own.

From the time I was with FedEx, I've been in the business of serving. And guess what? Something interesting happens to you when you're sowing seeds of service: you are served. Give and it will be given to you. Seek to live a principled life based on substantive things, and you're going to reap what you sow. That is very significant for me. It was behind my thinking about getting into business for myself, and it became a big part of my business.

I knew a guy who owned a business that audited freight shipping charges. He was sixty-five years old, looking to get out, and I convinced him, because I was a good salesman, to sell me his business with nothing down—just based on trust. This goes to show how important your reputation is. Whenever I worked with people, I tried to do it with integrity. I made sure they knew I was giving them my dedication and skill, that they could trust me, that they would get service from me above and beyond. I wanted people to know I was working on their behalf, and serving them in a way that I would expect to be served as well.

This guy was going to carry back everything. After the deal was done, I went to the bank and borrowed on the assets so I could give him a cash down payment. That was a leveraged buyout, even though I had never heard the term before. All I knew is that I had faith and hope that I could make this thing happen.

We started doing some unique things in the transportation industry. We specialized in finding freight overcharges and getting money back for our clients. . . . Serving. I did what I do best and spent my time leading the marketing and sales effort by personally going out to companies like General Motors, Ford, and Chrysler, just to name a few. From that I realized we were finding just as many undercharges as overcharges. So we approached the railroads and offered to find and recover undercharges in their freight billing.

After getting the Union Pacific Railroad Company as a client, I began thinking, *How am I going to get all of the data and information I need for the job, and how am I going to manage it?* So, in 1987, we got heavily into new technologies. I began to build one of the largest networking systems in St. Louis so we could do this job. We built a LAN, a local area network, at the very beginning of the era of computer and workstation networking.

I began to think about ways to improve our audit processes using emerging technologies—intranet, extranet, and LAN systems.

The question was: Was I in the technology business? Or was I in the business of changing the way people do business? We were going through a technological revolution—we still are, and it is changing the way we do business rapidly. I wanted to be a part of that revolution. Evolving out of that in 1990, I started this company called World Wide Technology to help do business in new ways—developing and deploying IT infrastructure for our corporate clients.

At the start I had four or five employees and no business, except we were able to secure one piece of business from a group at AT&T that would take a risk on us. That was the beginning of World Wide Technology. We were just a start-up, but one of my favorite passages in scripture says, "Call those things that be not as though they were." The power of our words is such that if we say that it is, it is. When we named World Wide Technology, we believed beyond our circumstances. We believed in this company one day becoming a mega-company. We thought of it as big in our own minds. Even though you couldn't see it, we saw it, and so we named it World Wide. In fact, we looked at a number of names. We talked about "St. Louis Computer Services." We talked about "National Computer Services." But "World Wide Technology" cuts across a lot of technology, cuts across the world. The more I think about it, it should have been "Universal Technology," but World Wide fits us well. We are now a global company providing technology to every corner of the world. Today, overall, the company this year is doing about $2.6 billion in business. We have 1,200 employees and some of the best back-office technology in the world.

But best of all, you walk through here today and you see people full of joy and excitement about being here, all working together, and it happens to be a company owned by a person of color. We've cut across all color and group divisions. That's really our strength. It is the hallmark that sends a resounding message to our community, both white and black, that we've done something special, and it's a model for others to follow.

## MAXINE CLARK
### Founder, Chairman, and CEO, Build-A-Bear Workshop

Maxine Clark is the kind of executive to whom others gravitate. She genuinely likes people and enjoys hearing their ideas. She is open, interested, and caring.

Clark brought these special traits, along with a flair for creative marketing and merchandising and an innate sense of fashion, to the retailing world, where she rose to the top in a male-dominated industry. She made a name for herself at the May Department Stores Company and then "arrived" when she was named president of Payless Shoes.

Throughout her retailing career, Clark has always been interested in providing her customers with rich, inviting consumer experiences. This is epitomized at Build-A-Bear Workshop, the company she founded, where young (and old) customers can design and build custom-made teddy bears and other furry creatures in "workshops" rich with atmosphere. Build-A-Bear started with a single location and now boasts over four hundred stores worldwide, including franchises.

Clark's career as an entrepreneur has its roots in a series of events that began at Payless Shoes, where she saw the retailing environment turn grim. It had quickly become a game of cutting expenses and competing solely on price, with no room for the creative approaches and quality products she felt would still win consumers' hearts. She realized that she no longer belonged in that world and knew she had to make a change.

As she examined the lessons she had absorbed from a series of mentors and teachers she encountered over the years, Clark looked for a way to exercise her own intense creativity and couple it with her business philosophy. When she found it, she was ready to make the leap into the world of entrepreneurship.

I was personally acquainted with two of the mentors who inspired and guided her—Stanley Goodman, former CEO of the May Department Stores, and David Farrell, also a former CEO of May. I know that they regarded her as a wonderfully gifted retailer. Oh, were they right!

————

THE PIVOTAL DECISION of my career occurred in January 1996 when I resigned as president of Payless Shoes.

When I joined the company four years earlier, it was pretty big news within the retailing industry. The executive ranks in the footwear business had long been dominated by men, even though women buy probably ten times more shoes than men. And so here I was, a woman assuming the top job of an industry giant, a chain that then had four thousand stores and $2 billion in sales.

I had a million ideas for Payless. I wanted to make it an exciting store to shop in as well as a wonderful place to find a great value. I think I did well, but the timing wasn't the best for someone who likes to use her imagination.

With the expansion of Wal-Mart, discount stores were being driven to the wall. Chains that couldn't find a way to keep cutting prices and keep growing at the same time could only go out of business. I knew Payless had to compete on price, but I believed that if we could make our shoes more comfortable and more fashionable that would also be more attractive to our customers. If our customers could pay $10 for a pair of shoes that looked and felt great, they wouldn't even think about going down the street to pay $7 for shoddy shoes at the lower-priced store.

If I had stayed at Payless, I'm certain I could have proven my point. But the culture within the industry and at my company was price-driven. To compete, chains would beat up on their vendors, demanding that they accept lower margins or cheapen their merchandise. I didn't want to be in that kind of business. I liked working with vendors, not ordering them around. Previously I found that I could trade ideas with vendors in the hopes of making each other more successful.

So I left Payless and the discount shoe business in 1996. I knew there would be interesting times ahead, but I had to remember who I was and determine what I wanted to do.

I am the product of two great teachers and one great business mentor. But first and foremost, there is my mother.

My mother died in 1972 at age fifty-six. Even so, I "speak" with her every day. A picture of the two of us sits on my dressing table. For my mom, Anne Kasselman, the world was painted in black and white. She had very strong opinions, and most of them were oriented around social justice and making the most of your time on this earth. You can do anything you want, she would tell me, but you are here to use your brain and make the world a better place. As I grew into a teenager, sometimes it was hard simply to be my mother's child. Could my mom possibly be so right all the time? I questioned that. I looked elsewhere for role models. I had to find out who I was and who would influence and give me confidence.

I found one role model in Marlene Adams, my high school journalism teacher. Where my mother took life so seriously, Mrs. Adams showed me you could pursue your interests and have fun doing it. I remember Mrs. Adams's boisterous laugh and her huge glasses. She was neither prim nor particularly ladylike. But as a journalism adviser, she helped her students over the years create one of the best newspapers in the state. As good as that paper was, Mrs. Adams each year gave her editors a fresh chance to reinvent it. And so we made our newspaper, *Highlights*, a living, breathing document that with each edition reflected our times. Because Mrs. Adams was so different, and successful, she made me confident that I too could take a different path.

I met my second influential teacher when I went to the University of Georgia, where I majored in advertising. There I met Robert N. Carter, a professor who specialized in consumer behavior and marketing. I learned from Professor Carter that price doesn't always drive sales: the environment you create for your product is just as important. But I learned something else from Professor Carter—perseverance. I was one of his best students, and I devotedly read everything he gave us, and I aced his tests. There were times he wouldn't call on me in class. Finally I asked him why he wouldn't. He answered, "I want you to get used to what it's like in the real world, when no one cares what you think." I owe Professor Carter a debt of thanks for teaching me that I would need a great deal of resolve to make my dreams come true.

Finally there's a mentor, Stanley Goodman, a legendary figure in the retail industry, who really fired up my imagination. He was a refined, dignified gentleman and always dressed impeccably. More often than not you'd find him in a suit with a square pocket hanky, a starched shirt, and cuff links. Mr. Goodman was a concert violinist, an art collector, and a highly successful retailing executive for the May Company.

And for some reason he took an interest in me.

I first saw Mr. Goodman onstage in an auditorium full of May Company buyers and executives. He talked about making the retailing experience a form of entertainment. We were the impresarios and the stores were our stage. We weren't just selling products, we were creating an experience. And if the experience was imaginative and entertaining enough, we'd never have trouble attracting an audience. Well, I had lots of ideas along those lines, and Mr. Goodman was kind enough to listen to me. He taught me to trust my instincts and believe in myself.

In the process of trying to figure out my next move, I heard all of these people telling me to start my own company. "Make it important," my mother says. "Make it different," Mrs. Adams advises. "Create an atmosphere around your product," Professor Carter implores. "Make it an experience," Mr. Goodman says. And then I can hear all of them saying in unison: "You can do it. We believe in you."

With all that wisdom, and lots of help from friends, colleagues, and coworkers, we opened our first Build-A-Bear Workshop in a shopping mall in 1997. In the last decade, Build-A-Bear Workshop has grown from that single store to four hundred stores worldwide. We built our concept on America's century-long love affair with the teddy bear—a very old idea. But we created a new experience around Teddy, asking guests to bring not just their wallets but their imaginations as well. You start by picking a furry friend, stuffing it, sewing it, fluffing it, and giving it a name. Build-A-Bear customers have now created millions of bears and furry friends in that way.

But ultimately I am my mother's daughter. Part of the bear-building process involves giving your new friend a heart. I wanted to make sure that our business had a heart as well—contributing something positive to the world. By 2008, Build-A-Bear Workshop's foundations surpassed $20 million in contributions to a variety of causes, including literacy, child welfare, and the environment. Our bears have been sent to soldiers overseas and to hospitals all around the world. I think my mother would agree—that's pretty positive.

# LEO R. JALENAK JR.
## President, CEO, and Chairman, Cleo Inc

Leo R. Jalenak learned early on that if he was going to get anywhere in business and be a good provider for his family, he would have to paddle his own canoe.

Jalenak found that canoe in the form of an ownership stake in a business called Cleo Wrap, a gift wrap company that he led into a $220 million business by the time he retired.

As a young man, Jalenak saw his father struggle to make ends meet for his family of five. His dad did not have a college degree, and his job at a New Orleans newspaper paid the rent but didn't provide enough income to allow him to purchase a home.

When Jalenak was a young teenager, his dad moved the family from New Orleans to Memphis to take a better job in a business owned by family members on Jalenak's mother's side of the family. In time, Jalenak took his place alongside his father in that business.

Working among his relatives, Jalenak thought he had found a solid, dependable platform from which to grow professionally and provide a secure financial future for his family. But an incident one day at the company headquarters changed all that. Jalenak was forced to realize that his sense of security was an illusion and that without some equity in the company—some piece of ownership— he would never be in control of his life or his future.

Energized by a motivation that many would-be entrepreneurs experience—the overriding need to be master of his own ship, to sink or swim based on his own knowledge, judgment, and decisions—Jalenak took action. With his move, he eventually was able to build the value of his company and increase his own net worth. Over the course of his career, he realized his goal and enjoyed the sense of control and security that had eluded him up until the incident that was his defining moment.

I WAS FOURTEEN years old in 1944 when my dad was asked to move
to Memphis—we were living in New Orleans at the time—to work
for his brother-in-law and a whole bunch of other family members
who were in business together. They had bought a company called
Mills Morris Company, which was a distributor of automotive parts
and appliances. My family moved up to Memphis in January of 1945.
As a teenager, the move was a big shock to me.

While going to high school in Memphis, I also worked at
Mills Morris on weekends and holidays. I worked in the shipping
department, at the front counter, and anywhere else they wanted me.

After high school, I went off to college, went to graduate school,
joined the air force, got married, and came back to Memphis to
work for Mills Morris. It was what was expected of me, and I didn't
think too much about it. Plus, the job was there and ready for me.

I started in the sales department and worked my way up to sales
manager in the Memphis territory. Memphis was the home office;
there were maybe twenty-five to thirty branches throughout the
mid-South.

In 1959 I was enjoying my career at Mills Morris. I felt I had
learned the business, and I wanted to continue in it. But at the same
time I felt that somehow I needed to get an ownership stake in the
company. The business was owned by my uncle and his brother-in-
law and other family members. My dad had a very small ownership
stake, and I had none whatsoever.

One day I was out making a sale to the Memphis Transit
Authority. It was a pretty large sale for a lift that raises buses so
that a mechanic can work underneath the bus. It was a multi-
thousand-dollar sale, and it happened to be on the same day that a
management meeting was scheduled.

Well, I couldn't leave the Transit Authority until after the sale was completed. Once it was completed, I rushed back to the office but got to the management meeting late. All my colleagues and other family members were there, including my father. The family CEO asked me why I was late. I told him about the big sale I had just closed, and he said, "That's no excuse. You're fired."

It seemed like an overreaction to me, but that's what he said. I left the meeting and went into my office, feeling shocked and embarrassed. An hour or so later, he came to see me and admitted that he had overreacted. "You're not fired. I'd like you to continue working here."

The incident made me start to think seriously about the Golden Rule. Not the one about "do unto others" but—no joke—the one that says that those who have the gold are the ones who make the rules. I decided that I'd better start looking for something different. I went to night school and took courses in real estate because I actually liked real estate a lot. I got my real estate license and became associated with a broker, and I did all this while I was still working at Mills Morris Company for the family. Only my wife, Peggy, knew about my interest in real estate.

But then here's what happened: I was doing some civic work for the Better Business Bureau, and one day I called on a friend of mine, Charles Wurtzburger, who was a business owner, and I tried to sell him a membership in the Better Business Bureau. It was a $50 membership. He told me there was no way he could afford that.

I said, "Charles, I know you. I know your quality of life. I know you can afford this."

He replied, "No, I can't afford it. The reason is that I'm putting everything into this new business."

Then I explained to him the benefits of having a membership in the Better Business Bureau, and why it was necessary for him to have a membership and be part of the Memphis community.

He gave in and agreed to buy a membership.

Then he said, "You know, you're a pretty good salesman. If you ever think you might want to make a change, please come see me."

Well, the next day I went to see him.

He told me all about his current business and the new business he was starting. They had been a paper and packaging jobber, and now they were going to move into "converting," making Christmas wrap, tissue, and kraft paper. They were going to sell to variety stores, drugstores, supermarkets, and other retailers and to other jobbers as well.

He made me an offer to join him in the new business. The offer included a 10 percent ownership stake in the business and a much larger annual income than what I was making at the time. I also figured out that day what my real value on the job market was.

I thought about it for a day or two, talked it over with my father-in-law and with a friend who knew Charles well, and I made the decision to make the change. It was very tough for me to tell my family about it, and especially tough because I enjoyed so much working with my dad. But it was time for a change, and this looked like a good opportunity to make one.

Deciding to leave the family business and get into something different turned out to be the most significant decision of my career.

I didn't see this as taking a big financial risk because I had no net worth to protect. Instead, this was giving me an opportunity to grow an ownership stake and to start over in a business that had tremendous growth potential. I still have the first contract that I signed, assuring me of my personal stake in the business. It is framed and hanging on the wall in my office.

The name of the new company was ultimately called Cleo Wrap (and later was changed to Cleo Inc). I started out in sales, did some traveling, and then became sales manager, then vice president of sales and marketing, then executive vice president.

The exciting part about our business was that we were on the cusp of a big change in the retailing business. Back then, you would purchase an item at a department store and could have it gift-wrapped. Sometimes stores charged for the service, sometimes they didn't, but there was nonetheless a cost attached to that service and the employees who provided it. Customers soon found it more convenient—and most times less costly—to wrap their own gifts. That opened up a huge market for Cleo at places like Walgreen's, Sears, and Kresge's (later to become Kmart). Cleo was among Sam Walton's first vendors when he went national with Wal-Mart. I was the guy in charge of getting those stores to carry Cleo's products. And as they gained more confidence in us, they began to handle an increasing line of products that we developed, including gift boxes and bags, ribbons and bows, calendars, and juvenile Valentine's cards. The company continued to increase its market share thanks to our strong national vendor relationships, and we ended up having the largest market share in the U.S. Soon we became attractive to corporate suitors.

In 1962 Charles sold 25 percent of the business to two large financial institutions in New York, giving us an influx of capital. Then, in 1964, the business was sold to CIT Financial Corporation, which owned Gibson Greetings, and we became the gift wrap division to go along with the Gibson greeting card division.

The company grew under Charles's leadership and, with my supporting work, continued to grow. Then, surprisingly enough, in 1974 Charles decided to retire. He was young, only forty-nine, and I took over as general manager, and eventually became president and CEO. I was also on the board of Gibson. When Gibson went public on the New York Stock Exchange in 1983, that of course turned out to be a good move for me, the managers, and the owners. It worked out well.

My career with the company lasted thirty-three years. During that time we had wonderful growth. We went from $1 million in sales in 1960 to $220 million in 1990, when I retired. Needless to say, I'm glad I took that step away from the family business and went off on my own. I relished being master of my own fate. At the time of my decision, I couldn't know how things were going to work out. I did know that having control of my future felt right. Looking back, it's the one aspect of my entire career that I couldn't do without.

# CHAPTER 3

# Love and Marriage: Finding or Shedding Business Partners

Meeting the right people and forming the right relationships in life might be fate, or it might be dumb luck and good timing. We all have lots of relationships: colleagues, bosses, spouses, friends, teachers. A good relationship can bring you up and a bad one can pull you down. Business partnerships are no different. Look no further than the executives in this chapter who say that finding the right business partner (or, in one case, getting rid of the wrong one) was the defining moment of their successful career.

Business history provides many examples of great partnerships. In fact, it's interesting to speculate on whether Microsoft would have become the giant that it is today if Bill Gates hadn't partnered with his friend Paul Allen to found the company back in 1975. Or look at the history of Apple. The charismatic Steve Jobs and the computer genius Steve Wozniak each brought different, powerful capabilities to Apple when they started the company, resulting in a legendary success story.

Some people spend more time with their business partners than anyone else in the world, including their spouses, kids, and friends.

No one will doubt that having a wonderful family and great friends enriches our lives immeasurably. Finding the right business partner has pretty much the same impact. For a personal relationship to work . . . well, that's beyond the scope of this book. But for a business partnership to work, I've found there are usually four imperatives: aligned goals, complementary capabilities, compatible personalities, and an explicit mutual understanding.

Having aligned goals means that the basic objectives of the business are the same for all parties. I'm not talking about empty statements that everyone can agree on, like, "We want to make as much money as we can." It's really about how the business will be managed, where it wants to go, and how it will get there. People and companies usually act rationally, and that means acting in their own self-interest. No problem there—we all do it. In a partnership with the goals aligned, if one party acts in his or her own interest, it benefits both parties. That's a good outcome. You're not just banking on a statement or a contract to keep things in check, but on human nature.

Profit-sharing or shared ownership is one way to help put goals into alignment. In my company's pharmacy division, we had the pharmacists take a 20 to 25 percent ownership stake in their stores. This gave them the incentive to work hard and do what was best for the company. The pharmacists felt vested in their business and were given a lot of authority over the operations and personality of their store. I remember walking into one of the pharmacy stores early one morning to find the pharmacist on his hands and knees scrubbing the floor. Now, I know that we had a good nightly cleaning service, so I'm sure the floors were just fine. But this guy was a perfectionist and was going the extra mile. If he hadn't been a part owner in that store, I don't think he would have been scrubbing floors that morning. We had common goals and this worked to benefit both parties.

A lot of people go into partnerships assuming that their goals are completely aligned, but after a while it becomes clear that the partners have different plans in mind. Maybe one partner wants to work hard, build the business, then sell it or maybe slow down personally to start a family; another partner wants to drive the train as fast as it can go for as long as it can go. Sometimes one partner is more of a risk-taker than the others. This might sound like a good counterbalance, but wait until the risk-taker wants to go into a deal that risks a significant portion of what everyone else has worked for. These kinds of disconnects often lead to a split because the partners can't agree on where the business is going.

Building a team with complementary skills and qualities is another key factor, and one that is often overlooked because most of us are more likely to entrust our business to people who are like ourselves. But companies don't need a team of clones, no matter how good they are at something. In the most successful partnerships I've seen, the partners bring different skill sets to the table. One person is more creative and the other more financial, or one is great at managing customers and the other is great at managing operations.

Companies understand this too—they look for corporate partners that complement their core competencies, markets, business processes, distribution channels, and so on. One of the executives featured in this chapter, Gyo Obata, illustrates how he and his partners leveraged their complementary skills from the beginning. To Obata, this was so important to the success of his company, HOK—now one of the largest architectural firms in the world—that the act of establishing from the beginning an innovative division of responsibility for him and his partners became his defining moment.

While differences in capabilities are an asset, differences in attitude can be a red flag. Whether or not the partners have compatible personalities might be difficult to determine upfront, but it is as important as any other factor. And for individual partnerships especially, mutual and complete trust is a must. I don't care how great an opportunity is, I'd never want to go into business with someone I didn't trust implicitly. Of course, if everything goes extremely well, trust might never become an issue one way or another. But virtually all businesses and partnerships have problems along the way—and you don't want to be in the lifeboat with someone you're afraid to turn your back on.

A business partnership really is like a marriage. It is intense. And while there's probably nothing less romantic than a prenuptial agreement, the business equivalent is strongly encouraged. Any prospective business partner who recoils at the suggestion of explicitly stating roles, responsibilities, and goals or planning for contingencies in the event that things go awry might not be the right partner. The longer a partnership goes without a common understanding of how to handle different circumstances, the more fertile the ground for dysfunction, and left unchecked, dysfunctional situations can evolve into bizarreness that is accepted as normal.

When a partnership is in the courtship stage, everything looks sunny and bright. The room brims with positive energy. Whiteboards are crowded with colorful sketches showing expanding market share, and PowerPoint slides animate how industries will be revolutionized. Who wants to spoil such a happy scene by calling in the lawyers? Believe me, I find it as painful as anyone to write checks to lawyers—but I've never regretted putting a tight agreement in place with business partners. Whether it's roles, responsibilities, expectations, or obligations, the more details the better. I've learned this both the easy way and the hard way.

The easy way because I've said countless times, "Thank goodness we had that term in the contract." I've also waited nervously by the phone to hear my lawyer say, "Yes, we contemplated that situation, here's how it's handled."

And then there's the hard way—when you don't have a road map to deal with a bad situation. One time we decided to launch a new retail concept, a deep discount drugstore. We had done our homework and business planning and the opportunity looked promising. We also knew it would take a different set of skills to run this kind of operation compared to running a conventional store because all the buying, receiving, merchandising, operations, and controls took place at the store level and the gross profit percentage was very thin. Strong management and ultra-efficient operations were critical. We looked outside the company for executive management and hired an executive with fabulous credentials. He had a great résumé, impeccable references, and relevant industry experience: he had run a similar type of store in another region of the country. He interviewed well and everybody liked him. We offered him the position, celebrated, and moved him and his family to town. Then the clouds rolled in. In my opinion, he simply was not up to the task. His marketing and advertising strategies, cost controls, inventory management—they were all wrong. We started losing a lot of money quickly. We had to let him go, but unfortunately we had nothing in the contract that anticipated such an exit. It seems pretty obvious, but we didn't cover it. So we bent over backward to be fair and simply paid him not to come to work for the course of his contract.

If good fences make good neighbors, then good agreements make good partners. Detailed contracts not only protect the parties but also guide the relationship.

The most successful corporate partnership my company ever engaged in was with a company called Sanus, a health maintenance organization (HMO). There was a high degree of compatibility between the companies and the people. In particular, I really liked and respected Sanus's chairman, Howard Waltman, for his business smarts, leadership, and honesty. When we were negotiating the deal to start Express Scripts, I went to New York to meet with Howard. He and I completed the deal while sitting at a table in Wolfie's Delicatessen, which was near his office and the only place we could go where we weren't getting interrupted. I wrote down the structure of the agreement on a paper napkin and we shook hands. Wouldn't it be a great story if I said I trusted Howard so implicitly—which I did—that the napkin still serves as the original agreement? But then I wouldn't be taking my own advice. Of course I went back home and gave the napkin to my attorney, who wrote up a good, detailed contract.

From thirty thousand feet, this partnership worked because the four critical elements were met. We had aligned goals, complementary capabilities, compatible personalities, and a detailed mutual understanding. It also helped that we had a good business concept too.

The stories of the executives in this chapter illustrate how important partners can be. With the right partners, you can carry each other up the mountain. And the wrong ones—well, they can send you tumbling down.

## MICHAEL STAENBERG
**Cofounder and President, THF Realty Corporation**

M ichael Staenberg has worked hard all of his life. In fact, he has been working hard since he turned eight years old. His father once hired him to clean out the basement, but then paid him only half of the promised amount. "We're partners," his father explained, and the rest of the money would go to help pay for food and rent. It was a lesson the young man never forgot. After his dad died, the family had very little money. Staenberg remembers that a shopping trip to Kmart or Woolco "was like going to Saks Fifth Avenue."

Staenberg's work ethic has served him well in his real estate ventures over the years, in some unusual ways. Rebounding from a disastrous market in the late 1980s, he worked tirelessly from four in the morning until midnight every day to liquidate his properties and repay every one of his investors. This salvage operation, and the stand-up manner in which he handled his responsibilities, led him to his eventual business partner, Stan Kroenke, who became instrumental in Staenberg's later success.

Now the head of THF Realty Corporation, Staenberg presides over a large realty firm that includes the development, investment, ownership, and operation of real estate properties throughout the country. The firm manages or owns more than 25 million square feet of property in retail shopping centers.

Staenberg's credo is: "Show up every day. Work as hard as you can. Keep blocking and tackling." He is the first to admit that he is as intense, driven, and impulsive as a man can be and that those traits can sometimes be destructive and counterproductive to good business. It was only through the good influence of his business partner that he was able to harness these behaviors and put them to use productively and successfully.

---

I GOT ACCEPTED to Stanford University and I was planning to go there. But one day in my senior year a friend of mine said, "You know, let's go to Phoenix and visit Arizona State. I'm thinking about going there. Do you want to drive down with me?"

I said, "Sure, why not?"

So we went there, and after looking around I started thinking, *Nice-looking girls—drinking age is eighteen—looks like a fun school—everyone seems much happier than at Stanford.* I thought, *By God, I'm going to go here instead.*

The first day at college I met a guy named Jim Nathan. He became my buddy. He had a car and I didn't, so that's what attracted me. We were college roommates for three and a half years. In our senior year he said to me, "What are we going to do when we graduate?"

I said, "I don't know." I had a job offer, and it was a lot of money, but I had long hair. I didn't like to wear a lot of shoes. I'm thinking, *I can't wear a suit every day.*

Jim said, "Let's go into real estate." I took a real estate class and kind of liked it. Then I remembered that I had a fifth cousin in Kansas City named Irv Maizlish who was in real estate. I called him up, and I said, "You know, I'd like to come talk to you about a job." He said, "We don't pay any commissions or any draws." I said, "Okay. I'm gonna come and just do it. I know I can do this. I'm smarter than everybody. I know I can be a salesman."

But I really didn't know what I was doing, and in my first year I made $2,200. Second year I made $7,900, which is not a lot of money. I'm thinking maybe I did the wrong thing. One day I'm looking through the Yellow Pages, and I get to the restaurants section. I see ads for McDonald's. So I decide to call McDonald's on a Monday morning and see if they want me to represent them.

I call their regional headquarters in St. Louis and get a guy named Mr. Blessley on the phone. I say, "Mr. Blessley, Mike Staenberg. Hey, how you doin'? I'd like to do some McDonald's deals."

The first question he shoots back is, "Have you ever done a McDonald's deal?"

I always told the truth—that way I couldn't get into trouble. It's hard for people to do that—it's hard for people to say, "I don't know," or, "No, I've never ever done that."

I replied, "No, sir, I never have, but I'm willing to work."

"Perfect," he said. "You gave me the right answer."

I ended up doing over 250 McDonald's real estate deals for this guy.

I met a man named Stan Kroenke while working on one of these deals. He was kind of a competitor because he was also in the commercial real estate business, but we became friends. At that time I had no idea who he was.

Through the McDonald's deals, I also met Sam Walton, founder of Wal-Mart. I ended up buying a piece of land that Sam owned, an out parcel in the parking lot of a Wal-Mart store, and then putting a McDonald's on it. Sam Walton was so happy with the deal that he told their director of real estate to "give that young man some business. He's done a really nice job. I'm impressed by what he did." So I started doing real estate deals for Wal-Mart.

One day I'm talking to Stan Kroenke, and he tells me that Bud Walton was very impressed with me. I said, "Who's Bud Walton?" He said, "Well, he's my father-in-law." Turns out Bud is Sam Walton's older brother and the cofounder of Wal-Mart. All I could say was, "Wow!"

Anyway, I had a lot of ups and downs in the business and had to work day and night to clear up debts that resulted when the tax laws changed in 1987 and the value of our real estate went down dramatically. One day I was a millionaire and the next day I was more than $20 million underwater. At this time people I knew in the real estate business, including the person who founded the company I was working for, were moving to Florida and buying multimillion-dollar homes because Florida tax laws were such that you could never lose your home. That's not how I was brought up, though. If you had a debt or obligation, you faced the music. And I did. I began to work out all my deals. To help me out, Stan Kroenke lent me a million dollars, and another gentleman in town did the same. Neither asked for any collateral or personal guarantees. They just said, "We believe in you." It took me years, but I worked out every deal I was in and made good on my obligations.

Then, in 1991, I went to Stan and said, "I'd like to do some deals with you."

He said, "Well, I really don't want a partner, but if you'd like to come work for me, I'd be happy to have you. Look, you find a deal, and we'll do it."

I found a deal in Pennsylvania. It was a very big deal with Wal-Mart and was going to include a Wetterau Food Store. I needed to put up $50,000, but I didn't have it. So I went to Stan, and I said, "You know, if you put the money up, we'll work out a partnership verbally—you know, on a handshake." The next day Ted Wetterau called me. He said, "Mike, I understand you were in Pennsylvania looking at a land deal. We have an operator for the food store. I'll tell you what. We have good news for you. We'll put up all the money, and we'll be partners." I called Stan, and I said, "I've got good news, and I've got great news."

Stan said, "What's the good news?"

I said, "Well, the good news is that I don't need your money. And the great news is that you're still in the deal on the same basis. Because I came to the dance with you, we're going to leave the dance together."

That was the first deal that started THF Realty. We were sitting around a table, and Stan said, "What are we going to call this venture?"

I said, "Well, I'm not big into names. The last three or four years haven't been a lot of fun. All I want to do is have fun. So we'll use three initials—THF—To Have Fun. People really won't understand what it means, but you and I will."

And that is how it started. My initial investment was zero. We started a leasing and management development agency. Stan and I each owned 50 percent of the corporation. I am president and Stan is chairman. We hit it big-time when Wal-Mart began expanding rapidly. I had a lot of development experience. We started with one shopping center in Kittanning, Pennsylvania. Today we have 125 shopping centers and 25 million square feet.

When Stan and I became partners, that was the key event in my career. I'm very driven, very impulsive, very fast-paced. I make decisions fast. Stan taught me patience. He taught me to sit back and maybe not react so fast. Try to be a little kinder to people, try to look at their side of things and not always judge.

The most important decision I ever made was deciding to team up with Stan.

## GYO OBATA
### Founding Partner, Hellmuth, Obata, and Kassabaum (HOK)

As a young Japanese American living in California at the start of World War II, Gyo Obata endured the painful and humiliating experience of having his family and friends forced into war internment camps.

Through his father's efforts and the intervention of powerful friends, Obata was separated from his family, avoiding the camps as they could not. Needing to leave California, he went to the Midwest, where he could finish school. He launched his career after the war and became one of the leading architects in the world.

As a founder of Hellmuth, Obata, and Kassabaum (now called HOK), Gyo Obata worked with his partners to build one of the largest and most acclaimed architectural firms in the world. By taking on a diversity of assignments right from the start, the firm avoided being associated with any one type of building and instead developed a reputation for versatility. HOK became equally adept at designing schools, airports, museums, corporate headquarters, sports venues, and hospitals.

Now the largest U.S.-based architectural firm, HOK boasts over two thousand employees, twenty-four offices on three continents, a reputation for listening to and understanding its clients' needs, and a portfolio of award-winning buildings.

What was the key to the firm's success? The three founding

members came together in a partnership of complementary skills and talents that allowed them to pioneer a novel—and clearly successful—approach to their work.

———

I GREW UP in California. I was born in San Francisco, and my family moved to Berkeley when I was in the fourth grade. My father was an artist and a professor at the University of California, where he taught painting. My mother was a floral designer who taught ikebana, a Japanese art of floral arrangement, all over the state of California. So my background is being the son of two artist parents, both from Japan. They were a big influence on my life in many ways—and they taught me about Japanese culture.

As I was attending Cal (the University of California at Berkeley) studying architecture, the war came, and all of the Japanese Americans on the West Coast were sent to internment camps. First we went to a racetrack, where they set up families in horse stalls, then eventually to permanent tarpaper shacks in the deserts of Utah. I think there were about twelve of those camps. They posted notices on the telephone poles in Berkeley and everywhere else in California saying that anyone with Japanese ancestry will report to a certain place on a certain date with just one suitcase.

As soon as we heard this was happening, my father said it was crazy, it was racial prejudice, and that he was going to try to get me away from there. He learned that I could avoid the camps and attend a midwestern college if a college would accept me and if I could get permission from the provost marshal, the person in charge of the military police. By that time I couldn't even go from Berkeley to San Francisco without getting permission from the army. My teachers at Cal said that Washington University had a very good architectural school, so I applied and they accepted me. I was about eighteen at the time.

So we went to the provost marshal for permission to leave, and the major we talked to said, "Oh, son, go along with Uncle Sam, and he's gonna take good care of you." He wouldn't give me a permit to leave.

My father was really enraged and went to the president of the University of California, Robert Sproul, who was a good friend of his, and said, "Can you do something to get my son out?"

Sproul made a call, and the next day we went to the colonel who was above the major who had turned us down, and he gave me permission to leave. The night before my family was to go to the internment camp, I left for St. Louis. It was a really tough time, but it taught me that you must always look forward rather than backward.

I went by myself, and I was one of the first Japanese Americans accepted by a midwestern school. A lot of colleges had already passed resolutions saying that if the Japanese Americans are dangerous in California, then they're dangerous here and we're not going to accept them. But Washington University has always had a very good civil rights record. About three or four years ago, someone showed me a letter where the chancellor at Washington U. went to the architectural school and asked the students if they would accept me. Fortunately, they said yes. By the time I left the West Coast, there was a real feeling of war because of the blackouts and the internments. In St. Louis it felt like there was no war going on, and that was very important to me.

Once I got through Washington University, I went to study for my master's with Eliel Saarinen, the father of Eero Saarinen, who did the Arch in St. Louis. This was at Cranbrook Academy of Art, a small graduate school for artists and architects located in Bloomfield Hills, Michigan. I got my master's there in architecture and urban design and planning.

Then I was drafted, but I only spent a short time in the army, as this was near the end of the war. Luckily, when I got out, I worked for Skidmore-Owings-Merrill in Chicago. They were one of the largest firms in the country at that time. I went there as a fresh rookie, and I worked there for about three years. Then there was a firm called Hellmuth-Yamasaki-Leinweber that had heard about me and wanted me to come and work for them in Detroit. I moved to Detroit, but most of the time I was working out of their St. Louis office. Then, in 1955, Mr. Yamasaki got sick and wanted to close the St. Louis office.

What happened next would set the direction for the rest of my career. That's when George Hellmuth, George Kassabaum, and I became partners and decided to form our own architectural firm and stay in St. Louis. A significant aspect of the partnership was the business decision we made to give each of the three partners a very distinct part of the operation to run. I would be in design, Hellmuth in marketing, bringing in projects, and Kassabaum on the production and construction side. Forming our company in this unique way—unique in 1955—made us much stronger than other firms because a partner really concentrated on his main area of responsibility, and it really helped us grow. It also differentiated us from our competitors. We realized that architecture is really a collaboration effort of many people because it's like redesigning the wheel every time.

We began our practice during the postwar period of school building. We started with elementary schools, high schools, and colleges. But another important business decision at the time was that we determined we didn't want to be classified as "one building"–type architects. So early in our career we also went after a wide variety of projects: corporate buildings, hospitals, prisons, anything you could think of, because we wanted a practice that was much wider in range than other firms.

We wanted to be able to put a whole building together from scratch. We realized we had to have very good urban planners, landscape architects, interior design people, and graphic artists. So we brought in people with many diverse talents, all of which helped us grow.

We were in St. Louis, and we were getting a lot of regional work, but we didn't want to be limited to the Midwest. We opened offices in San Francisco and New York. Then we gradually opened offices all over. Since then, we've designed airports, museums, hospitals, universities, courthouses, office buildings, laboratories, and churches. We learned early on that by having a wide variety of projects, if there was a downturn in one type of building, other types of buildings would keep us busy.

But in the 1970s there was a real recession in our profession because the entire country experienced a downturn. We looked overseas for work, and Saudi Arabia, at that time, was really building. We went after a university and an airport there. We were told that if we were going to do business in the Middle East, we would have to make payoffs. But we never did, and we still got the projects. One of the things very important to me was ethics. You always have to be honest and direct and never take any bribes or offer any.

The experience in the Middle East taught us how to work away from this country, and eventually we opened an office in London, and from there all around the world.

Wherever we are, I think it is important to always work toward building a better community, city, or region. Architects, as a profession, have a real responsibility to do good projects that are going to bring some meaning to the people who work and live in those buildings. That's what we've always tried to accomplish. I'm very proud of the buildings I've designed. Everyone always asks me, "What's your favorite building?" I always say that every one of them is like a different child. As an architect, I have to design buildings for clients. I think it's really important, say, for young architects to really listen to the client, rather than trying to tell him or her what to do. Listen first, and then you'll have all the opportunity to really do a good design.

Understanding and listening, I think, are among the greatest strengths that I have brought to this firm.

# JACK C. TAYLOR
**Founder, Chairman, and CEO, Enterprise Rent-A-Car**

When Executive Leasing (the precursor company to Enterprise Rent-A-Car) started in 1957, it was a very small, very informal affair. At any given time, the company would stock no more than ten or twelve cars—five or six Ford Country Squires, because they were really hot at the time, plus a few Chevys. The cars would be kept ready for any corporate customer who needed a vehicle quickly and delivered to whatever city or town where they were needed.

From these humble beginnings, Jack Taylor grew his automobile leasing firm into Enterprise, the largest car rental company in North America. Taylor pioneered the placement of rental offices in neighborhood locations, avoiding competition with the airport rental agencies. In 2007 his company acquired National Car Rental and Alamo Rent-A-Car.

It's probably safe to say that none of this would have happened if Taylor had not, at the beginning of his career, found a willing partner—Arthur Lindburg, who first hired Taylor as a salesman in one of his automobile dealerships.

Beginning as a salesman, and gifted with an eye for new business, Taylor began to notice that his boss was selling vehicles to a firm in Oklahoma that would then turn around and lease them to customers. Convinced that he had seen the future, Taylor teamed up with the boss, Mr. Lindburg, and Lindburg's two sons to found Executive Leasing.

It started off well, but as happens in many partnerships—even those that find success—the relationships eventually soured. Taylor knew that something had to be done. He confronted the issue head-on and in doing so could have easily destroyed the growing company. Instead, he encountered his defining moment.

———

I'VE ALWAYS LOVED cars. I started my first business around cars. I bought a used Chevrolet panel truck and went into the delivery business after serving in the navy. This was in 1946. I was twenty-four years old. I charged between twenty-five and fifty cents to deliver a package. After a few years, I had three vehicles and a couple of guys working for me full-time and several of them part-time, and I was making a decent living.

I was friendly with Earl Lindburg, whose father, Arthur Lindburg, owned a Cadillac distributorship in St. Louis. Mr. Lindburg offered me a job, and at first I turned him down. I said, "I've got a nice little business, and I don't want to give it up." One day Earl called and said, "Hey, Dad wants you to ride out to the airport with him." On the way out to the airport, Arthur Lindburg told me that the automobile business was expanding, and he was looking for a smart, young guy, and he thought I should come to work for him. He offered me $400 a month, which was about a hundred dollars a month more than I was making with my delivery business, and I was working seven days a week. I always loved automobiles, so I said, "Well, I'll give it a shot."

I went to work for Arthur Lindburg as a car salesman at one of his distributorships. I ended up running it but moved on to the main distributorship because my friend Earl wanted me down there with him. And that is where I was first exposed to car leasing and eventually started the car-leasing business.

A friend of mine had a leasing company in Tulsa, Oklahoma. Mr. Lindburg was selling him cars to lease. I went to lunch with him to find out what he was doing. I thought about what he told me and thought to myself, *You know something? With a deal like that, everybody's going to be leasing cars someday.* The beauty of it from the customer's point of view was that it was like a no-down-payment purchase—the customer could take his money and invest it somewhere and still have a car. From my point of view, I could lease all kind of cars— Cadillacs, Fords, or Plymouths. And I wouldn't need an inventory of automobiles because I could buy them as I needed them.

I wanted to get into the leasing business, so we started the Executive Leasing Company in 1957 with $100,000. At the time I was making about $24,000 a year selling cars, and back then that was serious money. When I told Mr. Lindburg I wanted to go into automobile leasing, he told me we were not going to make any money in this business. I think he offered me $750 a month to focus on the leasing business, which was less than half of what I was already making. I told him I couldn't live on that, but I felt I could make it on $1,000 a month plus my 25 percent interest in the company. He said, "Okay."

There were four investor-partners: Arthur Lindburg, his son Earl, his son Clinton, and me. We each had a 25 percent interest in the company. Everybody put in $25,000. I told Mr. Lindburg that I only had $10,000, but that I'd go out and put a mortgage on my house. He said, "Don't do that, Jack. I'll loan you the $15,000." He looked upon me almost as a third son. He knew I was hardworking. I considered him to be my mentor, and I had a great admiration for him. When we started the company, I thought I was the general manager. But one day Mr. Lindburg said, "Jack, call yourself the president." From then on, I was the president.

The business grew fast. In the first few months we leased about 25 cars. The next year we leased approximately 350 cars. We would carry about 10 or 12 cars in stock, in case someone wanted a car real quick. After five years we had between 1,000 and 1,500 leased cars. In 1962 we started the rental car division.

We were a local company until 1962. I had a young man working for me who was doing a pretty good job and was an eager beaver. We had been thinking that our concept could work in other cities, and I told him, "Okay, you want to grow with us? Here's some money. Go to Kansas City and Atlanta and come back and tell me which city you'd want to be in." I wanted the next city to be within a day's drive of St. Louis, so if we had inventory problems or used-car problems, we could drive back and forth in a day. He came back and picked Atlanta, and so we opened a second office in Atlanta in the fall of 1969. We also changed the name of the company to Enterprise.

Eventually, I bought the Lindburgs out of the business. Early on, Clint Lindburg, who was the youngest son of Arthur Lindburg, was worried that we were borrowing a lot of money and we were all personally guaranteeing the loans. The two Lindburg sons had some money, but the senior Lindburg would be looked to for money if there was some sort of serious financial problem. Clinton said, "I don't like personally endorsing all these loans. I'm not involved in the business. I want out." So we bought Clinton out. For his $25,000 investment, we paid him $114,000. There were now three owners, and we each had one-third of the company.

Then Arthur Lindburg started having serious health problems. He developed cancer. In planning his estate, he very generously gave Earl two-thirds of his share and gave me the other third, and he paid the taxes on the gift. That was a hell of a gift. I point that out to everybody because I want them to know how generous he was. I think he did that because he knew I was deadly loyal to him and worked hard for him. I really admired him. He was a terrific guy. He could be a mean bastard on occasions, but he was a good guy.

So now I had about 40 percent of the company, and Earl had about 60 percent.

Unfortunately, Mr. Lindburg and I had a falling-out over an issue. He got mad at me, and we eventually made up, but it was never quite as good as it was before. At one point I went to Earl and said, "Earl, your dad is pissed at me. I'm a 40 percent owner of the business. My son Andy is working in the business now. I think I would like to buy your interest down to where I have control. Or if that doesn't work, I would like you to buy me out, so that I can take my money and go with Andy and start a new business."

Earl said, "I don't know how to run the leasing business. I've never been involved. Let me see what Dad says."

He went to see his dad, and his dad said, "Well, I wouldn't sell out to him, but if you want to, then do it."

I bought Earl down to 25 percent. I had the rest, but with the understanding that when either one of us died, the other one had the right to buy the company. This was in the early 1980s. One of the toughest things I've ever had to do was to go to Earl and say, "I want control or I want to be bought out." It was a big decision to go do it, and there was a lot of risk for me.

As it turned out, Earl predeceased me, and I bought his 25 percent, and that's how I ended up owning the entire company. He died in 1989, and at the time we were a moderate-size company. We probably had 25,000 rental cars.

I took a risk. If Earl had bought me out, both Andy and I would have been out of a job, and we'd have had to start all over again. Probably, I would have been bought out for about $3 million at the time. With the money, Andy and I would have gone out and started another leasing company.

After that, Enterprise really blossomed. I've often thought that being freed up to make my own decisions was a big factor. One of the major decisions I made was to go into national TV advertising, which we did in about 1989. That decision really kicked us up the hill.

Another thing we did was handle replacement cars for people who had accidents. It's called insurance replacement rentals. We went to the insurance companies and said, "Why, when you have an insurance loss, do you make these customers either go without a car or actually make them go out to the airport and get a car from the airport car rental people? We'll provide a car in town for them. We'll see that they get a car—we'll actually pick them up." They agreed, and so we went after that market—we developed that market. About the same time there was a law passed in the Carolinas that said that when you have an accident the loss of the use of your car was a loss to you and the insurance company is obligated to reimburse you for the use of a rental car. And that created the market. We were now doing more short-term rentals than leases, so we changed the name of the company to Enterprise Rent-A-Car.

In the 1990s we decided the corporate market looked good, and we decided to get into it. We started providing cars to corporations, eliminating for them the need to own their own cars. Their cars basically were used only when they had executives or salesmen in town and would otherwise sit idle for periods of time. We would bring the car to the office when the executive or salesmen arrived.

My son Andy runs the business now, and I try to stay out of his hair. He is doing a better job of running the company than I could. When we moved to the new headquarters, I stayed in the old building. I didn't move because I didn't want to be there in the background second-guessing Andy. I wanted Andy to run the company himself.

I think about why some businesses expand and why some businesses don't. And I think the problem is often that a guy starts a small business and it becomes successful, then he thinks that nobody can do as good a job as he can, and so he won't delegate. But I have no problem with delegating. I had young guys that I brought up in the business, I trained them, and I sent them out to run our offices in other cities. I knew they thought the way I thought or I wouldn't have sent them out there. I had confidence in them, and the fact that they were making decisions on their own didn't bother me.

Today Enterprise Rent-A-Car is the largest rent-a-car company in North America. We are now bigger in the number of cars and more profitable than any of our competitors. Our revenue will be close to $13 billion with the acquisition of National and Alamo, and we now have more than one million cars. I keep asking Andy, How are we going to pay for all these cars? And he says, "Don't worry, Dad, we've got it covered."

# CHAPTER 4

# Betting the Farm: Risking Success for More Success

Being in business is being at risk.

Granted, it used to be easier to tell the secure companies and industries from the risky ones. If the financial crisis that started in 2008 told us anything, it's that the ground can shift quickly in ways that fundamentally change the economic landscape. Our largest banks and our most established insurance companies, firms whose core competency should be managing risk, found themselves on the wrong side of their bets and suddenly became the high-risk names in the business section.

Businesspeople take risks for any number of reasons. Some go looking for it, chasing the big opportunity. Others simply accept it as part of the business landscape, taking calculated risks only when necessary. Then there are situations or crises that demand a response; it's not a question of deciding whether a risk should be taken, but choosing which risky path to take.

In the drugstore business, we were a reasonably sized regional player, and that gave us some advantage in our markets given our size, buying power, presence, and marketing, but because we were still smaller than the national big boys (Walgreen's, Rite Aid, CVS), we always had to take more risks to keep up. Ever since Adam Smith and the beginnings of capitalism, we've known that competition benefits consumers. I can attest to that in our business. When the larger chains started moving aggressively into our markets, we had to respond. They could always beat us on price if they wanted, given their superior buying power with suppliers. We had to counter their advantage with innovative concepts or fast-growth markets where there was less competition. Some of our innovations worked (mail-order prescriptions, vision centers, adding food items to our store mix), and some didn't (deep discount drugstores, dedicated hearing aid stores), but in each case we took a chance, made an investment, and gave consumers more choices. Then they let us know with their pocketbooks what they liked or didn't like. And in each case—whether it was a winner or a loser—I could feel good about taking the risk, because I knew why we did it and I was prepared for success as well as failure.

I would not consider myself a risk-seeker, but I have never shied from taking a business risk, even a large one, once I fully analyzed the situation, knew the goals and pitfalls, understood the downside, and planned the contingencies. Only then could I take the risk and still sleep at night. On the occasions when I did not adequately perform due diligence, I was a nervous wreck.

I know a lot of businesspeople who are good gamblers. I really like the gamblers because they are far more interesting than "analyzers" like me. For pure drama, who wants to hear from the number cruncher who hyperanalyzes a situation when you could be regaled instead by the guy who makes up his mind on instinct and says, "Damn the torpedoes, full speed ahead"? One thing I have learned, though, is that you have to be comfortable in your own skin. If you're not a gambler by nature, don't try to act like one—it'll eat you alive.

Many businesses attempt to manage their risk proactively by envisioning different scenarios and "gaming" out the possible results. The role of strategy is to control the factors you can and try to make certain scenarios a reality. Strategy is also about estimating the probability of certain events happening and taking into consideration the possible impact of outside events. In business, tough decisions based on uncertainties need to be made all the time. Should the company expand? Make an acquisition? Adopt a new marketing strategy? Adjust price points? Change the product mix? Forge new relationships? What the people in charge can't do is shy away from necessary decisions that involve risk.

While I was a group president at Pet, we needed to fill a top position at the company. Two very qualified, road-tested candidates were vying for the spot. One was a smart, conservative guy who made good, thoughtful decisions, rarely made mistakes, and rarely took risks. The other candidate was also smart and analytical; however, he had made several high-profile mistakes. I awarded the second guy the job. He was not afraid to take risks, nor did he avoid taking the blame for bad outcomes. I felt that he could handle challenges better and take advantage of opportunities more quickly. It turned out to be a good decision.

Some of the executives in this chapter responded to crises by taking significant risks. In one story, taking the risk wasn't necessitated by events, but the potential payoff was large. It should come as no surprise that this person was Monty Hall of TV's *Let's Make a Deal*. I have also included one story—a cautionary tale—from an executive who took an unnecessary risk that did not pay off and whose venture, in fact, was an unqualified loser. On the positive side, that failure did motivate the risk-taker to dust himself off, get back in the game, and succeed—which might be the most valuable lesson of all.

# MONTY HALL
**Creator, Host, and Owner, *Let's Make a Deal***

M onty Hall grew up poor. As a child in Winnipeg, Canada, he saw his father toiling to support his family by delivering meat to butcher shops in town. His family lived below the poverty line, and they moved constantly to cheaper and cheaper housing as their fortunes declined. Monty would have never even gone to college if not for the intervention of a local benefactor. Offering to finance Monty's education, the businessman set down five rules:

1. You must keep a B+ or higher average.
2. Come and see me every month with your report card and talk about how you're doing.
3. You must never tell anybody where you got the money.
4. You must promise me that you'll do the same for somebody else someday.
5. You must pay me back someday.

Monty Hall never shied away from hard work and risk. During college, he worked nights at a local radio station. Then he moved to Toronto to try his luck in Canada's largest market as a radio announcer. His ambitions eventually led him to New York, where he knocked on doors in search of his big break. But no doors would open for him. When occasionally they did, the man behind the desk would usually say something to the effect of, "Oh, do they have radio up north? I thought the only things up there were the Royal Canadian Mounted Police and hockey players."

Monty couldn't catch a break, but he kept trying. Eventually, in 1955, the break occurred when a program manager at the local NBC station in New York took his call. Monty had been sending everyone he could think of in the television industry a one-page note called "A Memo from Monty," filled with stories about his adventures in New York the previous week plus a joke or two. Apparently the program manager had been reading and enjoying them, and he was willing to speak to Monty.

Monty began working in television and in 1963, along with his partner Stefan Hatos, created the most successful game show in TV history—*Let's Make a Deal*. The show featured Monty offering a variety of deals to members of the studio audience, who would dress up in costumes in an effort to get noticed and selected. If a contestant made the right choice, he or she could win a trip or other exciting prizes, but a bad choice would leave the contestant with a booby prize, such as a donkey, called a "zonk." The show was an instant hit, but Monty's deal with ABC gave the network most of the money. Unwilling to let that continue, he decided to take on the network. It is tempting for me to call this gambit "Monty Hall's Big Deal"—which, in many ways, it was. Suffice it to say, it was his defining moment.

I have known Monty Hall for over twenty-five years. He is a humble and compassionate man who deserves his success. He has devoted himself to charitable work and has raised millions of dollars for good causes. His manner and generous spirit are contagious—somehow, in sharing his work and subsequent success, he inspires others to want to do good and kind things as well.

———

I GRADUATED FROM the University of Manitoba in Winnipeg, Canada, in 1944 and decided to take an extra year of school. I was going to school in the daytime and got a job at a radio station at night. I worked from six to eleven every night at the station. I'd go home, get some sleep, and get up in the morning and go to school. After graduation, I worked full-time for the station. One day the manager of the station calls me in and says, "Here is a map of Toronto," and he hands me this map. He says, "You will notice that I put little marks on the map. Those are where the radio stations are."

And I said, "Yes?"

He said, "Well, there you are, so go."

I said, "What do you mean go? Do I have a job in Toronto?"

"No, you don't have a job; you'll have to go find it for yourself."

I said, "Are you telling me I'm fired?"

He said, "No, no, I'm not firing you. I'm telling you, you've got a lot of talent, and I don't think you should stay in Winnipeg. You should go for the big market in Toronto."

Toronto was the biggest market in Canada. I was twenty-four years old, and I belonged to a boys' club. Everyone pitched in a dollar and I was able to buy some luggage. I had enough money to get train fare, and that's about it.

I traveled to Toronto and ended up getting offers from three different radio stations as an announcer. So I'm doing radio broadcasting in 1946, 1947, 1948, '49, '50, and '51, and I'm just making a living. But television starts in 1952, and I'm in at the ground floor. I get a television show in the first year. I have a radio show, I have a television show—things are looking great. All of a sudden, the television show was canceled, and I spent a whole year looking for a job in television, and there was nothing available.

I made enough money on the radio show to keep the family going, but I was very disappointed, because television was my medium, and here I was doing one show and I was going to start a second one, and all of a sudden, no shows. And that's the way it was with the CBC, Canadian Broadcast Corporation. They didn't want to build any big stars. If you got too big, you'd want more money. They just canceled people right and left and then started with new ones, and then canceled them and just kept cycling through people. That's why so many Canadians came down to the United States to find their future.

So I go to New York to try my luck. My wife, Marilyn, encouraged me to go. She said, "You go. I'll be the mother and the father to our two kids. You go and see if you can make it." In New York I walked the streets. I really couldn't get in to see anybody. Fortunately, I still had a little radio show in Toronto, which provided us with a living. I would go back to Toronto, record the show, and then return to New York to look for work.

Finally, Steve Krantz, the program director of the local NBC station, gave me my first break. I ended up getting a job as a commentator on a weekend program on NBC called *Monitor*. I stayed on with *Monitor* for four years. I also started getting a local TV show on Channel 5, and I was also doing boxing and wrestling and doing color for the New York Rangers hockey games. My first network show was a show called *Keep Talking* that lasted four weeks.

In 1960 I got a call from the people doing a show called *Video Village* on CBS. The producer says to me on the phone, "Listen, the man who is emceeing the show has a big domestic problem back in Los Angeles, and he is leaving immediately. It's a live show. It's on live every day, and I need you to learn the show tonight and then do the show tomorrow morning live on CBS." They taught me the show that night, and the next morning I went on live, and it was a great success.

In 1961 the show was transferred to the West Coast, and I moved to the West Coast with my family. I started to work on creating shows for TV, and in 1963 my partner, Stef Hatos, and I worked for months developing a new show called *Let's Make a Deal*. Stef and I owned the show together. We tried out the show anywhere we could get a group of people together, and everywhere we went it received a wonderful reaction. We first showed it to ABC, but they turned us down. We then showed it to NBC, and the audiences went wild over the format, but NBC's initial response was muted. Of the two men from NBC who came to see the show, the man in charge didn't want it, but his assistant said to him, "I love the show. You've got to make a pilot."

He agreed, and in April 1963 we made the pilot. We heard nothing until October, when we got a call from NBC telling us that their 12:30 PM time slot hadn't had a success in three years. They asked us if we were ready to take over that time period, and could we be ready by January 2. No previous show had lasted more than thirteen weeks in that time period. We went on and we were a hit. Creatively, that was the most satisfaction I ever had.

When we were in the final year of a five-year contract with NBC, we asked for a raise and NBC stonewalled us. ABC entered into the competition offering a large incentive. We signed on with ABC and the rest is history.

Our show was very successful. We had a daytime audience of around 12 million people. Then they put us on at night in the summer. And the nighttime show had even larger numbers.

We were a hit at night in the summertime, but come the fall they wouldn't let us go on. ABC said, "This is just for the summertime because game shows will never work at night." You don't have to be a savant to know what's happened since then. There are plenty of game shows on at night now. But they said it would never work, and they wouldn't put us on at night.

We had an offer from some people to put the show into syndication. My partner and I told my agent, "We'll stay on ABC during the day, but we want the right to put the show into syndication at night."

ABC said, "Absolutely not."

What happened next is the critical juncture in my career. My partner and I were sitting in my agent's office, and I said, "If they don't give us permission to take the show into syndication, we're not going to do the daytime version with them."

My agent said, "Are you crazy? You have to do the daytime show."

I said, "No, I'm not going to do it. We've got some power here. We're the most successful show they've got, and I want the freedom to sell the show for nighttime syndication."

When you syndicate a show, you can sell it to any station in any market that you desire. And the big money made in television is through syndication.

My agent shook his head. He said, "You're crazy, you're risking your entire career." My partner Stef Hatos said, "Monty's right. We'll do what he wants."

So we phone ABC, and this is the conversation:

"If you don't give us the rights to go into syndication, we will not be at the studio tonight to tape. You've got until 5:00 PM New York time to let us know whether we get syndication or not."

I got off the phone and you should have seen the look on my agent's face. Nobody ever talks to a network like that, ever! My partner and I went to my house in Los Angeles and we waited for the phone to ring. At 2:00 PM Los Angeles time (5:00 PM New York time), nothing happens. There's no call.

My wife comes into the room. She looks at the two of us and says, "Well, you challenged them and you lost."

At 2:20 PM Los Angeles time, the phone rings, and it's the head man of ABC calling me from New York. He says, "Okay, you win." But you've got to do one thing for us. You've got to let ABC be the syndicator."

I said, "Okay. I don't care who syndicates the show. We've had offers from other people, but we'd rather do business with you."

Then we went to the studio that night and taped our daytime show.

I risked everything I had—my entire career—on this one decision.

My partner said, "Monty, you are really gutsy."

I'll tell you now, that was an understatement, because I risked everything I had worked for on that day. But it ended up working out. Our show went on to become one of the most successful game shows in TV history. The daytime show ran for twenty-seven years—the syndicated version only a few years.

But I must say, to the credit of my partner Stef Hatos, he took the risk with me. We were partners for thirty years until he passed away. His widow is my partner to this day as we sell the show to other countries and to networks here for reruns.

## FRANK JACOBS
### Cofounder, Chairman, and CEO, Jacobs International;
### Cofounder and Former Chairman and CEO, Falcon Products

Frank Jacobs is an ambitious and hardworking man who is driven to succeed. At the same time, he is guided by a highly developed sense of ethics and a strong desire to serve his customers honestly and well.

Jacobs led his company Falcon Products from a start-up venture to a mature company with revenues of $330 million. Falcon was a manufacturer of commercial furniture for the food services industry, in particular fast-food restaurants. The company was honored as one of the top two hundred small companies in America by *Forbes* magazine and *Business Week*. In 1992 Jacobs himself was named entrepreneur of the year by *Inc.* magazine, Ernst & Young, and Merrill Lynch.

But Jacobs wasn't content with that level of achievement. He wanted to grow Falcon into an industry leader, a billion-dollar international corporation, and he was willing to take some risks to get there.

As Jacobs freely admits, at the moment that could have brought him close to his ambitious goals, his sound judgment and professional management skills abandoned him. He made some quick decisions based on intuition and ended up derailing his business and his career.

As any successful businessperson will tell you, you can't let your failures keep you down. Although this failure was a blow that left some deep scars, Frank bounced back and has used the experience as motivation. He analyzed his failures and learned from his mistakes. Recently, with his son, he started a new company, Jacobs International, which also manufactures restaurant furniture, but with its base of operations in China. Jacobs is back selling furniture all around the world and, once again, enjoying business.

----

MY DREAM WAS to have a billion-dollar international corporation. When I took the step that would have gotten me very close to that dream, well, it turned out to be the biggest mistake I ever made and, unfortunately, the defining moment of my career.

When I was discharged from the air force, I started looking for a job. I had a cousin who was a manufacturer's rep, representing a whole group of companies that sold products to restaurants. We decided to go into business together making table bases—the base that a tabletop sits on. We each put up $500, and we called it Falcon, which was the name of my air force squadron. Several months later, we got into an argument, and I gave him his $500 back, and I owned the whole business.

I was very lucky, getting into an industry that was the second largest in the U.S.—second in size only to the U.S. government—

and that was food service outside the home. It was when McDonald's, Kentucky Fried Chicken, and Holiday Inn were starting to grow, and I happened to start a company that was selling pedestal tables, which all these restaurants wanted.

At the time, the restaurant equipment dealers who sold to the chains were hungry for product. It was a seller's market: they would buy from anybody who could deliver. They didn't care who you were or what you were. If you could deliver three table bases to the side of a mountain on Thursday afternoon, that's all they cared about. And that's what I did. I'd get the bases built, deliver them, take more orders, and keep going. When things got busy, I hired someone to answer the telephone, and I hired another employee to help me pack. And that's how Falcon got started.

From 1950 to 1981, I didn't really make a lot of money from the company—I had to keep it all in the business. The company grew quite rapidly. I had to finance my accounts receivable and inventories. I did a lot of fund-raising. Banks wouldn't lend me money, so I had to learn how to borrow. I did factoring. Our industry was comprised mainly of small companies, and I used to say to myself, *This industry is going to be big business. It's ripe for someone to really grow.* My goal was to acquire these small companies and become a large supplier with a broad range of products to offer to the food service equipment industry.

Things went well, and in 1976 Falcon went public. It was a great way to raise money. I raised $1.8 million in our initial public offering, and the funds helped me acquire companies to fill out our product lines. Falcon picked up companies that made tables and chairs to go with its table bases. Through these acquisitions, Falcon became a total provider of an entire line of furniture products for the food service and hospitality industries: table bases, tabletops, wood chairs, metal chairs, and upholstery goods.

In 1981 Falcon was a $20 million company. I made my first

mistake when I decided to bring in a guy to run the business while I went off to focus some of my attention on an unrelated business opportunity. I spread myself too thin. It was a disaster and almost led to bankruptcy. But I came back and started running things again, made some better hiring decisions, and brought stability back to our financial and manufacturing operations.

At that point, I decided I needed to create a board of directors who were not my friends but were business experts. Things started going well again, and by 1999 we were a $150 million business.

With this success, I started thinking Falcon was ready to get to the next level—to take that big jump toward my long-held goal of a billion dollars. My next move turned out to be my defining moment. I made the decision to buy a competitor called Shelby Williams. I'd been wanting to make this move for a long time because they had a part of the market we did not have—hotels, colleges, health care facilities.

The day after announcing we were going to acquire Shelby Williams, Falcon stock had the largest percentage jump of any company on the New York Stock Exchange. Evidently the market liked the acquisition too.

This deal, however, put Falcon—one of the best companies in the industry—into a position where it was destined to fail. I did not have the management team, infrastructure, or systems to handle a company that had basically doubled in size. Also, we did not do a good job of due diligence. I hired new, outside executives to take over key roles, but it just didn't work.

The acquisition caused organizational, management, and financial problems and eventually led us into bankruptcy. For a while I resisted declaring bankruptcy. I wanted to avoid that in the worst way. I didn't want the shareholders to lose their value. I really believed I could fix things just as I had done back in the early '80s. Through the sheer force of my personality, my drive, my personal investment in the company, and my ability to raise money, I thought I could jump back in and make it happen. But actually it made no sense. We were much too large. The debt was much greater than it had ever been, and interest costs were too high. I finally came to the conclusion that the current against us was too strong. In retrospect, I should have taken the company into bankruptcy a year before we did.

In bankruptcy, though, I was operating in an environment I did not know or understand. Nevertheless, I remained optimistic we were going to take this company through bankruptcy, out of bankruptcy, and back to growing the business.

I made a deal that all creditors would be paid 100 percent, so that no one would lose any money. The shareholders would get 10 to 15 percent of the new company. We would have an opportunity to grow the company again, and to grow the stock based on a new balance sheet.

I put together a plan that looked good on paper, and I knew we could execute it. I was starting to execute the plan when I was hit with something I never expected: my board of directors had several meetings to discuss my future role in the company, and they told me I had to resign or they would fire me.

This was the company I had started more than fifty years ago. There was really no reason for this to happen. Maybe I wasn't thinking clearly. I owned about 20 percent of the company, and I could have walked back in and gotten rid of the board of directors. They wouldn't have stood up to me. But I didn't do it. I had been hit with something I never expected, and my knees buckled for the first time in my life. I just let it go. I wish I hadn't.

I still believe I could have stayed with Falcon, brought it through bankruptcy, and seen it operate successfully. It could have been a very good company again. But it didn't happen that way. I lost my money, my company. I lost it all.

I spent a lot of time trying to put this into perspective. I am no longer angry and confused about some of the things that happened. What I did know pretty quickly, though, was that I couldn't just sit around and worry about gaining perspective for the rest of my life. I had to keep moving, and I had to allow this experience to teach me a lesson. I've got a lifetime of valuable experiences in business—both good and bad—and I'm taking that knowledge and charging ahead again with a new company. I'll let the past teach me a lesson, but I won't let it weigh me down, not when I've got a new company to get excited about.

## JERRY FINGER

**Managing Partner, Finger Interests Ltd.; Former President, Chairman, and CEO, Charter Bancshares**

Jerry Finger was engaged in a number of ventures before going into banking, including real estate development, frozen food processing and grain storage, and the retail furniture business. He eventually chose banking because, in his view, it was a simple kind of business—at least it was back in the early 1960s. In Houston, where he lived, there was little price competition between banks because it was quite difficult to get a bank charter in Texas. A bank was almost an exclusive franchise. Finger was also attracted by the fact that at a bank management had to close the books at the end of every day. Thus, ostensibly, management always knew exactly where the business stood financially (except for the loan portfolio quality). He opened his first bank in 1963.

Finger grew his business smartly and carefully, and his bank survived the depression that hit Houston in the 1980s, when the price for a barrel of oil fell from $40 to $8. Most other large banks in Houston and Texas did not make it.

Throughout his banking career, Finger avoided quick, risky profits as well as rapid, unsustainable growth. And when he needed more money to grow his banking business, he did not take the usual route. For many entrepreneurs, the cost of new capital is giving up control of their company. Not for Jerry Finger. He fought to continue to control and run his company his way.

I have known Jerry for nearly sixty years. I know how he approaches business: he does what is right, not what is expedient. It might be a more difficult path sometimes, but over the long run it has served him and his shareholders well.

————

As a young man, I made some reasonable money in the real estate development business. Concurrently, I was a partner in a successful venture engaged in frozen food processing and grain storage. Our food venture received an offer to purchase the controlling share of a Houston bank. We spent almost a week on bank premises performing due diligence and then made an agreement to buy. Three of us went to the closing, but the person who owned the bank came to the meeting drunk as a lord, and thus we were not able to effect the closing. But I personally had discovered a precise objective—I wanted to start a bank and run it.

So I applied for a bank charter. Though I was young, I think the regional comptroller liked me, but at first turned me down. With revised data, I went back, and then, with further revised data, went back again. I finally received the charter.

People couldn't believe I got that charter. This was in 1962, and I opened the bank in 1963. Daddy and I put up the equity, and he owned about a quarter and I owned about a quarter. Together we owned 52 or 53 percent of the bank, and so controlled it. I had an option to buy his stock at fair value.

I named the bank Republic National Bank of Houston. The

largest bank in Texas at the time was Republic National Bank of Dallas. It was one of the finest banks in the country and was very well branded and respected. Texas then had no branch banking. I was able therefore to steal . . . uh . . . borrow their name.

We had a lot of shareholders, and we were able to grow fairly quickly. I grew the bank by being a good merchant. In other words, I advertised like hell and offered good services and products at competitive rates. In particular, I'll refer to the way we handled certificates of deposit. In the early 1960s, when the Federal Reserve, on a Friday afternoon, allowed the banks to raise the rate payable on certificates of deposit to 5 percent, I got in touch with my ad man. I met with him that same Friday night, and we had ads in the newspapers on Sunday—we advertised in Houston and the cities within 150 miles of Houston. Because we were small, I could make decisions rapidly. The big banks would probably decide to do the same thing—but they had to have meetings. It took them two weeks to move their CD rate up to 5 percent. I knew we had a head start, but in two weeks' time there would be plenty of competition. In spite of the competition, we were able to take the bank from $4 million in assets to $12 million in six weeks.

The key event in my career came a few years later, when the bank was growing and needed more equity. I didn't want to put it all up myself—I couldn't afford to—so I did a convertible preferred stock rights offering, giving the existing shareholders pro rata rights to buy convertible preferred stock or Class B convertible preferred stock.

The regular class preferred got a 7 percent dividend and could convert into one share of Republic National Bank common stock. The Class B preferred stock got a 3 percent dividend and could convert into one share of Republic National Bank Class B common stock that had rights to nine votes per share. Two small shareholders and myself bought the Class B preferred stock. I bought 99 percent of the Class B.

Now, the reason I pursued the matter that way related to
my experience in the Young Presidents Organization. YPO had
meetings in other parts of the country and other countries as well.
There was a meeting in Rio de Janeiro. I was chairman of the tennis
committee and met some fine men there. Many were older, though
others were near my age. But a couple of them were a lot more well-
to-do than I was.

I had already been pondering what to do about getting more
equity for the bank and about the possibility of having to give up
control, maybe going public. After a beer following a match, one of
the Brazilians I met asked me to visit him and his father in São Paulo.
I did. We talked about the bank and discussed the circumstances
relative to the long-term bank ownership. His father said: "You never
give up control." A senior YPOer from an old family in Mississippi
had said almost the same thing. Neither of these men would ever give
up control. They had accumulated a lot more experience than I, were
very successful, and spoke in the absolute.

Their advice impressed me so much that I decided to structure
the deal in the way I've previously described, with me buying the
Class B preferred. When I later sold stock to NationsBank and thus
owned only 40 percent of the then-common stock after conversion
of the Class B, I still had 52 to 53 percent of the vote.

That allowed me continued independence. One of the reasons
I didn't sell my bank or go to work for somebody else was that I
had to be my own man and could never have worked effectively
for someone else. It's always been that way. I was able to do what
I thought best for the bank and, further, I was able to take the
long view. I could look down the road being less concerned about
the earnings next quarter or even next year. That's why the bank
survived. Further, I was dealing in large part with my own money.

At one point, though, we were right on the edge. We had just
been through a bank examination, the best bank examination we

had ever had. The regulators said we were the cleanest bank they had seen in some while. But they suggested that we had become large enough that we ought to have our own internal loan review group. We hired examiners to do internal loan procedures, and I went off to vacation in France.

I was gone almost a week when I got a call from my senior lender. "Jerry," he said, "I've got some bad news for you." He explained that our internal examiners had reviewed the loans at the largest of our banks—by that time we had five—and determined that we had some bad real estate loans there and suggested we charge off or transfer to reserve $1.5 million for potential loan losses.

I was shocked. "A million and a half dollars? You're out of your mind."

"Jerry, that's what he said."

So I replied, "Okay, we'll do it." I did some quick calculations using a 45 percent tax rate, and thought: *Okay, it's bad, but we're still earning lots of money. It isn't going to kill us.*

Two days later my guy called back, and he said, "Jerry, he finished the examination and he thinks that we ought to charge off a total of $3 million."

I said, "Yeah? I'll be home tomorrow." I left France, got home, went through all of our banks, and ended up charging off or reserving $4.5 million. This was approximately a year and a half before all the other banks recognized their own bad real estate loans. At this time, we were listed on NASDAQ. The charge would change our quarterly earnings dramatically to the negative, so we sent the data to the SEC. We also called the Comptroller of the Currency and told him about it. He couldn't believe it either, because they had just conducted the examination. He sent down some examiners from up east and they cut us up like a melon. We had to charge off even more.

As a result, we did start cleaning up a year-plus before the other banks. Again, I did not care about the current earnings. I wanted the bank to survive the depression. We got out of real estate lending and tightened all credit decision-making. We foreclosed many real estate credits and sold the property as quickly as possible at the then-market price—regardless of the appraisal or the loss incurred on the sale.

And all that saved our ass. It's accepting reality and knowing how to look it in the eye. I was able to do it because I had kept my independence. Also, when the bank lost $2 million, $1 million had been mine.

In the late 1980s and early 1990s, we grew the company substantially. We purchased several failed banks from the FDIC and opened a number of new branches in Houston and surrounding cities. With less than normal competition, we were aggressive and successful as "new business getters." We *were* the largest locally owned bank in Houston. In the late 1990s, I sold the company because the buyer simply offered too much money.

## JOHN D. GRAHAM
**Chairman and CEO, Fleishman-Hillard, Inc.**

John Graham has always had the ability to keep his eye fixed firmly on the future. Early in his career at Fleishman-Hillard, he determined that the public relations firm could survive only if it won some big accounts and put its financial house in order. He focused on those twin goals and he achieved them.

Graham continued to guide the company with drive and prescience and can now rightfully claim that Fleishman-Hillard is the largest public relations firm on the planet, with three thousand employees working in eighty offices around the world, including three offices in China.

But it might not have turned out that way.

Back in the mid-1970s, Graham caught his first glimpse of a future that would favor the PR firms with national and even global reach. As a regional business at the time, Fleishman-Hillard was at a significant disadvantage when competing for larger accounts.

Graham's defining moment came with the realization that the firm had to expand out of its home market, where it was doing very well, and begin the march toward a national presence. Although knowing the direction of the future doesn't mean having the capability of getting there, Graham decided to risk everything in order to try.

We know the ending to this story—we know that Graham succeeded. But it turned out to be a bumpy ride, with a lot of twists and turns and near misses.

———

I JOINED THE public relations firm of Fleishman-Hillard in 1966. I had the opportunity to work on some great accounts, including Anheuser-Busch and Emerson Electric. By 1970 I was vice president, director, and senior partner, and in March 1974 I became president and CEO.

We were a small company back then. We had just one office, and it was in St. Louis. Bob Hillard and Al Fleishman were very happy to have the business located there.

There were a couple of issues that I thought were critical to the future of the business: we needed to secure some significant accounts and we needed to get the business in good financial shape. I focused on those goals for several years.

We opened our first office outside of St. Louis in 1977. It was in

Kansas City and was very successful from the beginning, primarily due to the fact that a woman we had working for us there was just outstanding. But it proved the concept to us that we could make other offices work, and it became obvious to me that we needed to have a presence outside of St. Louis and beyond the Midwest. That became my new focus.

Our challenge, however, was that we were a privately held company and did not have a lot of resources. I went to New York—I spent a lot of time in New York—and we finally decided we would open our own office there. A number of people in our industry told me, "John, you're a St. Louis–based company; you'll never make it in New York. You're from the Midwest—you don't know how New York operates."

That was a challenge to me. We did start an office in New York, and it was somewhat successful. Then, in 1982, two years later, I decided we needed to have an office on the West Coast. So we opened one in Los Angeles.

These were very challenging years. Still privately held, we didn't have a lot of financial resources to draw on, and I had to borrow money from the bank to keep the business running and growing.

The bank happened to be my client, the old First National Bank. It was a very difficult situation. I'd sit with a loan committee, and they would say, "Now, John, we understand your office in New York is just barely making money, you've opened an office in Los Angeles, and it's not making money. Now you want to borrow some money because you need to open an office in Washington, D.C.? And by the way, what do you do for a living?"

I ended up having to mortgage my home, and my CFO mortgaged his home in order to make payroll every two weeks.

It was in this very tough environment that we had to make the crucial decision: should we stay in St. Louis or should we go ahead, roll the dice, and take our chances with expanding and really become a national firm?

You know, St. Louis was not exactly the public relations capital of the world. As we looked at the situation and looked at what our competitors were doing, we knew we were not going to survive as a firm if we didn't grow. We would either be bought by somebody we didn't necessarily want to be bought by or we would go out of business. We knew we had to expand in order to compete—in order to keep the clients we had and in order to compete for new ones. In fact, I came to believe that we had to expand very fast if we were going to survive at all.

It was not an easy decision. It was risky to me personally and financially, and to a lot of other people as well. I mean, when you're borrowing money to make your payroll every two weeks, that's a risk and a big move.

It was an emotional time, but we didn't abandon rational decision-making. We didn't do it seat-of-the-pants. I had a planning committee, what might be defined today as an executive committee. We looked at the situation continually over a two-year period. We just kept looking around, doing a lot of fact-gathering, putting together a tremendous amount of information, and considering it all in our planning.

As we looked forward, looked at our numbers, and looked at our competitors' strategies, what we needed to do became very obvious to all of us—we had to go ahead and take the risk and expand.

If we failed, a number of us would have gone bankrupt personally, and not only that, the people who worked at the firm would lose their jobs. I don't want to sound like an old-fashioned shopkeeper, but I just felt responsible for these people—we had about sixty at the time—and I still do.

But we didn't fail. You know, a lot of success in our business has to do with momentum, and we managed to maintain our momentum. It's enabled us to recruit great people around the world; it's enabled us to guarantee to our clients that we can do great work for them no matter where they are in the world—whether in Brussels, or in Russia, or in India, or in Kansas City. That is really important to a lot of our clients. The work we do for 85 percent of our clients is done out of more than one of our offices. At least 40 percent of our clients are not based in the United States.

At a certain point we had to go international, and we opened our first European offices in 1987 or '88. The question for me then was, does our culture, which really grew out of the Midwest and our office in St. Louis, apply on an international basis? And I will tell you for a fact, it applies. It applies whether we're doing public relations or communications business in Beijing or in St. Louis.

We may have eighty-four offices around the world, but our Midwest culture, which is based on service to clients and respect for people, is evident everywhere. We teach the same basic values for every office, such as: respect for the individual; teamwork is everything; quality of service is first and foremost in everything we do; the business drives the firm; results make us go; existing clients come first; ethics requires a personal commitment; and, as a firm, we are committed to the highest ethical standards.

And it works. I'll be, for example, in a meeting in Beijing, and I will have one or two of our young people there tell me what they're doing, and they'll quote one of these values back to me. They'll say, "You know, existing clients come first, Mr. Graham."

And I'll say, "Yes, I do understand that."

# LEE LIBERMAN
**President, Chairman, and CEO, Laclede Gas Company**

---

Lee Liberman never meant to stay very long at the Laclede Gas Company. He joined the company without thinking much about it—Laclede's offices were close to the employment office that gave him the job referral, so he just dropped in for the interview. Once there, he thought he'd stay just three months and then go to law school. He had been accepted to Stanford Law School and was just looking for a way to make some quick money.

What looked like a cavalier attitude toward his career hid a true seriousness of purpose and a drive that Liberman put to the service of Laclede from then until the end of his career. He spent the next forty-six years rising to the top, eventually serving as president, CEO, and chairman.

Liberman believes intensely in the notion that the man in charge has a responsibility to make the tough decisions and stand by them—even in the face of opposition from some of the people around him.

In his defining moment, Liberman showed remarkable grit and resolve, taking action against an obstacle that he was convinced could destroy the viability of his company and jeopardize the safety of his customers. He took a great risk, putting himself and his business in harm's way, not just financially but in a physical sense as well. He won, and his company won—but at great personal expense.

---

I STARTED AT Laclede in 1946 and stayed until 1992—forty-six years. When I started, I got a big salary of $175 a month. I didn't know I was poor. With overtime pay, I was probably making a little over $200 a month.

My jobs included assistant to the president and chairman, and manager of the "street" department, where I had several hundred employees reporting to me. We did all the construction work, putting in gas mains and service. I next became superintendent of operations. They were training me to run the business, except I knew there was a lot of competition and it would be difficult to get the top job.

And then they put me over in the labor department, and I was eventually vice president of labor relations. That was a tough job, because we had a miserable union. If the union didn't like something, they would just walk off the job. That was illegal—they were breaking the contract we had with them. One of our VPs used to say, "Damn, what the hell's going on here? Are we running this company or are they running this company?"

The most difficult decision of my professional life has to do with that union: I decided a strike was inevitable—a five-month strike, as it turned out, and in the winter, which is the worst time for a strike because this is when we sell the most gas by far. And winter is when we have the biggest problems with the business. While many of the management people felt a wintertime strike was dangerous, they were mostly supportive. I felt that taking the strike was the only way I could get control of this company, but I was not a pioneer. We had had other strikes, and they always produced difficulty.

The union was the OCAW—the Oil, Chemical, and Atomic Workers. We were probably their biggest target. They used to walk out all the time. They would put water in the gas main, which was terrible and dangerous. They did it more times than I can tell you. If you put water in a gas main, your burners won't light. If people forget they have their burners on when we take the water out and the gas comes back, you can injure or even kill somebody. We had to go into a lot of the houses in the area and make sure that the burners were off so that we could put the gas back on. It was a mess, I can tell you.

They would even do things like that when there were no labor problems. They also turned a lot of houses off, things like that.

I had five hundred management people running the company during the strike, and none of them were in the union. The strike lasted five months, from October to the following March, with several thousands of workers out. It was not fun. The union would call my home phone constantly—all night long. One night I finally got the brilliant inspiration to just put the phone on forward and send all the calls back to the union office. They also turned the gas off in the building where I lived. I never knew how wild some of these people could be.

Letting the strike happen involved a lot of risks in terms of dollars, property, and of course there's the human risk. People could get hurt; we might not have been able to deliver on our obligations; we didn't know if we could service our customers, didn't know if we could make it through that long winter period with the union on strike.

My feeling was that the strike was necessary. I didn't have everybody agreeing with me, but one of the things I've learned is that when you are CEO you have to make that final decision. The buck really did stop with me. And if it didn't work out, I would have been in trouble.

During the strike, I spent a lot of time at the company, day and night. A lot of times I spent all night there. I lived there. I slept there. I was really emotionally tied up in the whole thing.

We won the strike, and after it was over we had love and peace. The union wasn't so demanding after that. Management was in charge of the company again.

The union was tough—really tough. But in the end, we had total peace and cooperation and an improved relationship with the union.

# CHAPTER 5

# Hearts and Minds: Creating a New Corporate Culture

I guarantee that if you were blindfolded and airdropped into Google's headquarters—known as the Googleplex—in Mountain View, California, you would know within ten seconds that you were not at Microsoft. And you would know even sooner that you were definitely not at IBM. Google's edgy office is punctuated with exercise balls in the hallway, lava lamps, and dogs sleeping on couches outside cubicles. IBM's Armonk, New York, headquarters reflects the rich formality of an older, more conservative, more traditional company. Its hushed corridors lined with expensive artwork, its tasteful displays of artifacts from the firm's illustrious history, give the place the air of a handsomely endowed museum. Its beautifully appointed boardroom with a gargantuan wooden conference table speaks to the firm's power and wealth.

Of course, there is a lot more to corporate culture than the appearance of a company's headquarters, although it is certainly a strong clue as to what the company perceives its corporate culture to be.

"Corporate culture" is a company's value system, its DNA, its personality. Corporate culture defines the shared goals that drive executives as well as rank-and-file employees. It determines which behaviors are acceptable and which are not. It encompasses a code of conduct that people intuitively draw upon when they deal with fellow employees inside the company and with customers or vendors outside of it. If you ever hear someone say, "That kind of approach is encouraged here," or, "That would never fly here," the speaker is probably referring to the company's culture.

Corporate culture starts from the top and is driven by management into all the nooks and crannies of the organization. Employees are always watching the CEO and senior executives to see if they really embrace and embody the declared culture and are willing to implement policies that make it come to life.

It's easy for the boss to say, "We're ethical," or, "We listen to employees," or, "The customer always comes first," or, "We give back to the community," or, "We believe in work-life balance," but if the company doesn't support such notions with policies and programs that, for example, value ethical conduct over profits, give time off for community work, allow parents to work flexible hours, or formulate meetings and processes that allow employees to have an impact on company practices, then it is all just empty verbiage in a memo or a speech (or, worse yet, a plaque). Companies that try to implement a culture as window dressing but don't really believe in it are exposed very quickly.

Culture has an impact on whom the company attracts, hires, and retains as employees. Cultures can be conservative or progressive, strict or relaxed. Companies that have tough, success-at-all-cost cultures attract and hire people who believe they can thrive in such a setting. People who work on Wall Street go there looking for something different from what appeals to people who work at the local bank. I know of a company that encourages every employee to take a one-month sabbatical every five years. You certainly won't find that on Wall Street. It isn't that one culture is better than another—it is merely a case of what works for a particular company.

Even companies in the same industry can have very different cultures. The first time I flew Southwest Airlines, I felt a little uneasy about the joking attendants, the polo shirts replacing dress shirts and ties, the short pants instead of slacks. But Southwest knew what it was doing: building a strong company culture and reflecting it in the brand. Would that same culture work for British Airways? Probably not.

One way to think about the role of culture is to look at the organization as a set of systems that must work in harmony with each other. Each of the company's systems—its business model, organizational structure, work flow and processes, policies, technologies, reward system, and culture—must support and complement the others. If one system falls out of sync, the organization doesn't function optimally. Culture, then, doesn't exist in a vacuum. If it doesn't support the rest of the company in the corporate mission—or, worse, if the culture is at odds with that mission—it will create problems or dysfunction.

As each of the executives in this chapter would confirm, corporate culture is probably the most difficult system to change because it is abstract, it is hard to define, and changing it requires changing people—their hearts, minds, behaviors, and attitudes. In contrast, when you change a business model, or enter new markets, or introduce new product lines, or cut operational costs, people know and understand what's happening and can adapt to the change. But when you attempt to put your thumb on corporate culture, you are trying to capture an intangible, even if ubiquitous, quality.

Sometimes an attempt to change the culture is an attempt to change the way people have approached their work for many years. Most people look at the changes being implemented for the good of the entire company and relate them strictly to themselves: *How's this going to affect me? How will it change what I do? Will it make it harder for me to get a promotion?* And generally people fear that change won't be for the better. Employees have to be convinced that change is good for them as well as for the organization.

Some people are unwilling to make the change. I once tried to work with an entrepreneur whose wine, spirits, and gourmet foods chain had been acquired by Pet. He was a smart, gregarious man who loved to hang out in his stores and interact with customers. Nothing wrong with that—except that's *all* he wanted to do. He had no use for the mundane (but essential) tasks involved in running an organization: administration, planning, budgeting, or even preparing his stores for future growth. No organization can be managed that way for very long. After trying for months to get him to adapt to the Pet culture and run his stores professionally, I reluctantly had to give him an ultimatum: if he wouldn't work with us, then, for the sake of his own company and its growth and prosperity, we would have to part ways. He agreed that he could never operate in the formal, professional manner our culture required, and he left. He was wrong for our culture, but he knew how to run a store and keep his customers happy. And that's what he did, once again setting up his own business, rubbing elbows with his customers, and enjoying the life of an independent store owner.

In each of the cases in this chapter, when the executive took over as CEO, he instinctively knew that the existing culture was an impediment to future success, and it was the first thing he attempted to change. Some executives had a notion of how to fix the culture, while others had to look outside the organization for answers, seeking advice and inspiration from some expected as well as unexpected sources: an elite global consulting firm, an academic, and even the Boy Scouts of America. Yes, as you will see, the Boy Scout Law played an integral role in shaping the culture of one of the most important companies in America.

Just how difficult is it to change corporate culture? Each of the CEOs in this chapter had a noteworthy and successful career. Each led his organization through good and bad times, grew his company to new heights, and made shareholders very happy. Yet when asked to identify the defining moment of his career, each pointed to the time when he turned around the corporate culture. These executives are most proud of their work in reshaping their company's culture precisely because it was such a difficult, yet absolutely necessary, task.

## SANFORD N. MCDONNELL
### Chairman and CEO, McDonnell Douglas Corporation

When Sandy McDonnell took over the reins of McDonnell Douglas from his uncle, the aircraft manufacturer had been dominated for many years by a management of one. His uncle, James S. McDonnell, had started McDonnell Aircraft and was the first CEO of McDonnell Douglas.

As James grew the company, he had retained the key decision-making power for himself. Sandy was very familiar with his uncle's command and control style. James was a strong and dominant leader who ran the show, gave the orders, and made the decisions. Sandy had also witnessed strong top-down management in his dealings with his largest customer, the Pentagon. But when Sandy took over the company, he realized that this type of management structure would serve neither him nor the company well and that it had to change.

To his credit, the younger McDonnell also realized that, unlike his uncle, he couldn't and shouldn't run the business on his own. He wanted to create a professionally managed firm where decision-making was delegated to those individuals in the best position to make the call and where the participation of many levels of management was encouraged. He saw the need for a system that would allow him to draw on the knowledge, talents, judgment, and decision-making abilities of others in the organization.

McDonnell understood that achieving this goal required a change in the very intellect of the organization, the manner in which every employee thought and acted—that is, the McDonnell Douglas corporate culture.

Under Sanford McDonnell's leadership, the company grew into the world's largest aerospace/defense company, with over 115,000 employees and revenues of over $13 billion.

————

JAMES S. MCDONNELL, my uncle, was the founder of McDonnell Aircraft and the first CEO of McDonnell Douglas. Everyone called him Mr. Mac. In 1972 I became president and chief executive officer, but I wasn't truly the boss until my uncle died in 1980. When I was appointed CEO, I found out quickly how the power was to be distributed. Just a few weeks into my new position, we had a disagreement on a business matter, and I said, "Now that I'm CEO, I'll take responsibility for doing it my way." Mr. Mac replied, "Sandy, there's something you don't understand. You may be CEO, but I'm still the boss." So it wasn't until I became chairman as well as CEO that I realized what it was like to really, truly be the boss.

My professional crucible was my decision, upon Mr. Mac's death, that I needed to make a lot of changes in the company—really to modernize its management philosophy in a way that would fit the capabilities I brought to that position. I felt strongly that there was need for cultural change because, while Mr. Mac was a genius, he also liked to do everything himself. I, on the other hand, was not capable of doing everything myself, and I knew it. We had to move from one person making most of the decisions to a corporate structure that allowed for growth. We needed a system that would allow more delegation and give us the opportunity to tap into the creative powers of everybody in the corporation to a greater degree than we had done with Mr. Mac.

I think that any change of management style and culture is difficult. It takes time, and it takes very careful timing and execution. People are afraid of change. Change brings unknowns, and people don't like unknowns.

At the time the most highly respected CEO in the nation was Reginald Jones, who was chairman and CEO of General Electric. I knew him vaguely and called him up and told him I'd like to come and spend a day with him—sitting at his feet, so to speak—to learn as much as I could about what he thought about my situation and what he would do in the way of making changes. He was very gracious in doing that.

I came back from that experience with a number of suggestions I wanted to institute. One of them was about the board. We had an inside board when Mr. Mac was running things, with only two outside directors. We changed that around, giving the majority to outside directors, who would be more objective in their view of our corporate affairs. Jones also recommended a strategic management program, which we went about setting up. He recommended a human resource management component, which we also set up. I got help on that from Chuck Knight at Emerson Electric.

We also set up what we called the "Five Keys to Self-Renewal." The self-renewal concept was based on John Gardner's book *Self-Renewal*, where he writes about how people are born, mature, and die, but that doesn't have to happen to corporations if they go about self-renewing. Then they can live on and on. So we came up with (I like to say "we"—the big "I" is something I try to avoid) the Five Keys to Self-Renewal, which were:

- Strategic management (planning, decision-making, controlling)
- Human resource management (a system for getting the best people and giving them opportunities to grow)
- Participative management (involving as many people as possible in the decision-making process)
- Quality/productivity (improving products and cost competitiveness)
- Ethics

I was really interested in ethics. Being active in the Boy Scouts as a young person and again as an adult with my son, I focused on the Scouting emphasis on character-building and ethics. That to me was the most significant and important "key." No matter how smart and good and creative a corporation or person is, if they do not live by high ethical values, in the long run they won't survive. So our fifth key was ethics, which I believe ran through everything and controlled everything we did: our relationships with suppliers, customers, and employees. In my view, ethics was basic to running effective management in the other four key areas.

In 1983 I gave two vice presidents the Scout Law ("A Scout Is Trustworthy, Loyal, Helpful, Friendly, Courteous, Kind, Obedient, Cheerful, Thrifty, Brave, Clean, and Reverent") and said, "I want a code of ethics for McDonnell Douglas that is a positive 'thou shalt' type of code, as opposed to a negative 'thou shalt not.' Every corporation has a 'thou shalt not' code. But they don't have a 'thou shalt' code."

We came up with a code that incorporated most of the points of the Scout Law. The only point it didn't incorporate was "a Scout is Reverent." As a Christian, I would hope all of our employees believe in God, but as a CEO I did not want to use my position to force them to be reverent.

This code of ethics was adopted unanimously at the April 1983 board of directors meeting. We then set up an eight-hour training experience, starting with me and my direct-report people, to teach how to apply the code of ethics in our daily business lives.

One thing I found when introducing the ethics program was skepticism among the employees. There was so much pressure to meet the bottom line that many felt that when push came to shove, management might not really put ethics above the bottom line. They felt that we would look the other way if it was necessary to cut ethical corners to meet goals and objectives. But over time people realized that we were not just talking about a code of ethics, but that we really believed in its importance and tried our best to practice it. We had to lead by example. If we hadn't, if the CEO didn't walk the talk as well as talk the talk, our sincerity would be questioned.

Over the years people came to me and others and thanked us for taking this position, because they felt it was a tremendous load off their shoulders to know that if it looked like they weren't going to meet their goals and objectives, we didn't want them to cut corners to meet them. They began to understand that if they came to us we'd be more willing to negotiate new goals, as long as they were reasonable.

Being ethical in everything you do is not only the right thing, it's also the smart thing. To treat everyone ethically—suppliers, employees, and customers—in the long run, you will not only survive but also prosper.

EXCERPT FROM THE McDonnell Douglas Code of Ethics, based on the Scout Law:

Integrity and ethics exist in the individual or they do not exist at all. They must be upheld by individuals or they are not upheld at all. In order for integrity and ethics to be characteristics of McDonnell Douglas, we who make up the corporation must strive to: (1) be honest and trustworthy in all of our relationships; (2) be reliable in carrying out assignments and responsibilities; (3) be truthful and accurate in what we say and write; (4) be cooperative and constructive in all work undertaken; (5) be fair and considerate in our treatment of fellow employees, customers, and all other persons; (6) be law-abiding in all of our activities; (7) be committed to accomplishing all tasks in a superior way; (8) be economical in utilizing company resources; and (9) be dedicated in service to our company and to improvement of the quality of life in the world in which we live.

# BENJAMIN F. EDWARDS
## Chairman and CEO, A. G. Edwards

The plot line of Benjamin F. Edwards's defining moment is remarkably similar to Sanford McDonnell's. A. G. Edwards and Sons, the distinguished brokerage firm, was founded in 1887 by General Albert Gallatin "A. G." Edwards, who served as assistant secretary of the Treasury under President Lincoln. The firm had essentially been a family-run enterprise since its founding. In Ben Edwards's early years at the firm, all decisions were made by his father, Presley Edwards, who not only ran a tight ship but controlled everything that happened on it. The elder Edwards would even go as far as checking every employee's work—including the details of every stock trade.

When Ben became president, not only was he carrying the

weight of a long and illustrious family involvement with the firm, but he was faced with a business whose growth had depended on the micromanagement of a strong leader. Like Sanford McDonnell in his family's business, Ben realized that the only way the firm could continue to thrive and grow was to wean it from its dependence on one-man rule and create a professionally managed organization and a new corporate culture. He reevaluated and altered a wide swath of company policies and procedures, including the reward and compensation system, stakeholder priorities, accounting practices, and hiring policies. He even modified his own behavior and role in the firm.

Ben Edwards's overhaul of the company's culture included the adoption of a mission statement that became critical to the reputation and image of the company in future years. It put the client first in every decision and action of the company, employees second, and shareholders third. When Edwards became president of the company in 1967, the company had 300 brokers and 44 offices, and when he retired in 2001, at the age of sixty-nine, the firm had over 6,900 brokers and 691 offices. In 2008 A. G. Edwards was acquired by Wachovia, which in turn was acquired by Wells Fargo in 2009.

Benjamin F. Edwards died on April 20, 2009, at age seventy-seven. He had a remarkable career, leading A. G. Edwards through its greatest period of growth. I knew him for over twenty years and can tell you that he was a man of the highest integrity and was very kind and very humble. He graciously allowed me to interview him even though his health was failing. Ben will be greatly missed.

---

A .G. EDWARDS was my great-grandfather. He was an assistant secretary of the U.S. Treasury under Abraham Lincoln. In 1887 he and his son—my grandfather—formed the brokerage firm that bears his name and has been in my family for over a century. The brokerage and banking firm has essentially been a family-run enterprise ever since.

My uncle William McChesney Martin joined the firm in the 1920s as the head of research. He went on to become our first floor broker at the New York Stock Exchange, and then he became the first president of the New York Stock Exchange. Later he became assistant secretary of the Treasury under President Truman, and then chairman of the Federal Reserve Board.

Jumping ahead to the mid-1960s, my father, Presley Edwards, and I are in the business, and he is running it. He becomes ill, leaves the company, and moves to Florida, so I became managing partner, and I held the job for forty-some years.

My father knew all the parts of the business, the operations as well as the sales. I didn't. He would come in really early in the morning and check every trade from the prior day, and he would spot mistakes and mark them. He had a color system, stickers and whatnot, and the employees would recheck the numbers before the bills went out to clients. People got so they relied on Press Edwards as the fail-safe here. I wouldn't have noticed a mistake if I stared at it.

We were a one-man show. We were growing, but if we were going to grow any more—and we certainly wanted to—running the company would be beyond the capacity of any one person, even if the person was twice as smart as I was. I figured, *I'm not going to be successful, and the firm isn't going be successful, if we rely on one person. Everybody has to do his job well.* I realized that I had to do something.

I think the single thing, my most important realization, was that we were going to have to implement a new management structure and have a mission that brought us together and had us working in the same direction. Once I realized that, then it was finding a means to do it.

Bob Lefton, a pioneering corporate and human development psychologist, introduced us to something called the "managerial grid," a behavioral leadership model that helped us establish candor and transparency throughout the company. It came out of the University of Texas. And I think the realization that we needed something like that was probably the only spark of light or genius I ever had. I did it by necessity, because I had to rely on other people.

We used the managerial grid for assessing ourselves, our communications, and the way we were solving problems. It helped us more critically evaluate the way we worked with each other and our clients. We had many people dealing with the same clients, and we all needed to be on the same page, trust each other, and act toward clients in a consistent and honest way. This required complete trust and candor among all of our employees, and a management process for critiquing each other to make sure we were focusing on what's best for the client. With this, we were able to build mutual trust and candor. And in the forty-some-odd years that I was at Edwards, I think you could count on one hand the number of people who let us down when they were trusted.

It took us two years to develop our management style and organization. We'd meet on Fridays in Fenton, Missouri, at a motel across from the Chrysler plant, and we would stay overnight, and then meet all day Saturday and come home Saturday evening. And we did this two days a month, every month, for two years. We didn't let anything just pass by. If we all agreed on something, we'd look at each other and say, "We missed something here, we shouldn't all be agreeing on this, we didn't look deep enough." And we'd dig into it until we really thrashed it out. We also ended up drawing up the A. G. Edwards mission statement.

We decided that we would unite everybody at Edwards and that we had one common purpose: doing all our work for the benefit of our clients. It meant that we couldn't keep the books to our convenience. Even though we were a partnership, we should book-keep just as though we were a publicly held corporation open to scrutiny by the public. All the policies and things we did should benefit the client. If they didn't, if it was just to benefit ourselves or some other party, we wouldn't even waste time discussing it. That policy turned out to be in forty years a very viable thing; it worked.

After that, it was the doing—we had to perform. We decided to continue the growth plan my father started. He thought the place for the small or even midsize firm was going to be a tenuous one in the business. We had to grow larger, and we did.

In our hiring priorities we looked first for character, and then we looked for talent. We didn't want the most talented person if no one could get along with him. And this worked in the long run, really.

Something that had become common in the brokerage business was to pay upfront money or bonuses to people to join you from other firms. We decided we would not do that—that wouldn't be fair to the people who were already working for us. But in terms of growth, our hiring policies really put the pressure on us. If we were to grow, people would have to think that we were a better place to work—a good team-oriented environment that would benefit them financially, and in all ways, in the long run. I knew we could become that better place if we put our priorities straight: the client, and then the employee, and then the shareholder, in that order. The brokers knew that their clients, who were their security, came before the shareholder. They liked that, and they liked the fact that we were people-oriented.

I liked to go out and visit branches. It was a great benefit to me because I really stayed in touch with the real world out there. With most of my counterparts, all they ever saw was the management floor of their headquarters. I got to know our people really well. I went to the branches not to give speeches but to ask questions:

"What could we do to make your job easier? Where are we screwing up?" I'd come back with my list of suggestions, and we'd talk about them in the department meetings. This made everyone in headquarters client-oriented too, because they were hearing from the brokers in the branches, who were closest to the clients. And that's how they were being judged. Even our research analysts, unlike most of the industry, were permitted to talk to our brokers and our clients directly.

Our compensation system was another important part of the cultural change. We decided that only the brokers, who were on commissions, and the managers, who had a percentage of the bottom line of their branch, would get a variable compensation. Everyone else got a straight salary, and it was a very modest salary, plus a bonus that was a share of the profits. Brokers and managers also had a portion of their compensation from the firmwide bonus pool. That way everyone benefited from the performance of the entire firm. We did it all the way down the organization.

In many years the bonus was by far the largest part of our compensation. But if we had a flat year or a down year, or we had one year where we barely made a profit, we didn't get any bonus. We figured that if our own personal compensation was dependent on the performance of the whole company, then there wouldn't be turf wars and people jockeying for position. If you ran a division and I ran a division, I'd root for you to do well because, if I was having trouble, you might be the one who made up for it and created part of my compensation, and vice versa.

So we were all pulling for each other. Even people who were totally different in every way respected each other's business talents and worked well together. People were sharing information, giving honest opinions, and working toward the same goals. This made us ready for growth, and the culture made all that possible for us.

## DAVID FARRELL
### President, Chairman, and CEO, May Department Stores Company

---

When David Farrell became chairman and CEO of May Department Stores in 1979, the company and industry were at a crossroads. New competitors and shifting trends were challenging the old business models; shopping centers were saturating the marketplace; families were moving to the suburbs (many of May's stores were in old downtown locations); and specialty retailers as well as discount stores were popping up and growing at a rapid pace. May was not keeping up with the new selling environment, and its numbers reflected it.

Farrell had another big problem. May had grown mainly by acquisition as the company purchased many family-owned department stores around the country over the years. Management control of this growing, disparate entity had not kept pace. For the most part, the families continued to run these businesses, and they ran them all differently and sometimes not very well. Many were weak in all vital areas: products, merchandising, presentation, operations, control. Because it remained so decentralized, May's management was unable to bring any kind of unified vision or strong direction to this collection of stores.

When Farrell took over, he instinctively knew this had to change, and that meant transforming the company from a collection of quasi-independent operations to a united company committed to a culture of excellence, high expectations, and high performance. His vehicle for accomplishing this was a plan called "the May Mission."

Farrell's defining moment came with the development and adoption of the May Mission. He turned to some of the best minds in management, the prestigious global consulting firm of McKinsey & Company, to help him develop the mission and plan for its rollout.

Consultants can provide sound and even brilliant advice. But when they're done with the project and the report is written, they move on to the next client. Often they are not there when the client begins to implement the plan, nor are they around for the aftermath, which is not always pretty. By using consultants, Farrell chose a direct but potentially risky path. He introduced a plan created "from above" by consultants and a small group of senior management and then asked everyone to support and implement a plan they did not participate in creating and had not been asked to approve. He knew he'd be swimming upstream, but his instincts told him that this was the only way to make a radical and necessary change in the way the company was run.

In total, Farrell was with May for forty-six years. When he started, volume was between $300 million and $400 million; when he retired, it was $14 billion. May was sold to Federated Department Stores in 2005 for $11 billion.

———

THE MAY COMPANY essentially grew through acquisitions. There was internal growth as well, but over the years we acquired a number of department stores, starting in Cleveland. They were established stores, and in many cases family-owned stores. Often, after May acquired them, a member of the owning family would become a director of the May Company. When Stanley Goodman [one of Farrell's predecessors] took over, May had a families-dominated board, making it difficult to govern.

I could tell you a lot of horror stories about the independence of the guys running the divisions, and the effects carried over for a long time. Having all these independent organizations was a big issue for us. We had a number of different families who originally owned the stores now operating them under different cultures, different philosophies, and in a very decentralized environment—very decentralized.

Rarely did management groups come together—or when they did, it was purely social, not for planning purposes, with each guy telling how good he was, how good his store was. Stanley Goodman started to change that. He started president's meetings, with agendas set by the corporate office, and began to try to pull together some parts of the company that would help in planning.

But each organization had its own set of systems for doing things, even their own point-of-sale systems. At that time bar coding was not around. It was just at the beginning of trying to track merchandise information by SKU [stock-keeping unit], and there were many competing systems for that in terms of point-of-sale devices. You had NCR, you had IBM, and a number of others. A lot of this was left to each individual store to sort out. Even the way we designed stores was left up to the individual store company. And at one point individual stores started getting into real estate. We'd have guys who were running the stores all of a sudden trying to negotiate deals with very sophisticated shopping center developers.

Eventually things started to happen. You realize you have to do things differently. As you sort through where you stand, you realize that you're a mediocre company in a mediocre industry. The financial returns for the department stores group really had become quite dismal. They had all become very unimpressive players, and that was something May had no interest in being a part of. It was with that realization we started to work on the May Mission.

If you decide your company has become mediocre, you have to figure out some way of moving ahead of the pack or out of the pack. As we looked at the industry, the only guy who was really doing it right in the department store field at that time was Macy's. Macy's was a very good operator with a very tight organization. It was operating in New York and San Francisco in a big way, and to a lesser extent Atlanta. But Macy's was really dominant. So you say to yourself, somehow, some way, Macy's was able to become a top performer, with a top return on investment. So, in looking at that, you realize—this was back in the 1981 period—you have to decide how to become a top performer as well. But how? How do you do that dance? We started saying, "Look, we have to do something. We just can't keep doing what we do here. And we're not going to buy our way out of this. We've got to operate our way out of it."

We started interviewing consulting firms to help us out, and we got lucky in some respects in that we got hold of McKinsey & Company. With McKinsey, we came up with the May Mission, standing for excellence in retailing. The whole process of developing and implementing the mission took the better part of two years.

We worked on it without the participation of operating companies, without people in the field. We did it with about ten or twelve of us. May as a company never liked big meetings, so when decisions had to be made, it was generally with a very small group.

The plan we adopted for achieving excellence in retailing had three main tenets. One, have the best talent in retailing. That's a trite statement in many ways, but we had to work like hell to bring in the best. Second, be innovative. And finally, attract superior general management. This did a hell of a lot for me personally in thinking about what May should be doing.

Fortunately, working with McKinsey and with the small group of executives at the company, we were able to understand better what the role of the CEO should be, what the role of the central organization should be, and where May was going. We began to adopt a traditional management structure with a strong CEO in a central organization with responsibility for planning, decision-making, and controlling.

We found clarity in terms of the corporate management: What does corporate management do? What are you responsible for? That was an issue that you'd say, "Well, gee, as I look back, that's not so hard to figure out." But it was.

We were able to move to a more centralized merchandising operation with the sense that you really had to make these stores alike, you couldn't be operating with all the stores being different.

The May Mission also set objectives. These dealt with productivity and involved specific, measurable goals that included improved sales per square foot. Objectives and strategies also covered merchandise impact, genuine customer service, sound pricing policies, vital sales promotion, visually exciting stores, efficient systems, and top performance. So that when you go through those strategies, they are a vehicle for bringing your organization together.

To implement the May Mission, I traveled to each division and spent many hours meeting with the merchandising organization. We had large meetings with the groups and went over the mission points. It turned out to be inspirational. The fact that May now had a document like this meant a lot to our people. I think everyone was very proud of what we had accomplished with the mission.

Once we were centralized, we were able to get things done. People began to understand what the central organization was responsible for and what the operating companies were responsible for. Some people in the industry said we were operating with a heavy hand. Federated Department Stores, for example, prided itself on the fact that it was decentralized and that there was a lot of autonomy in the company.

A lot of things changed at May, and with our new management structure we were able to acquire a hell of a lot of department store companies. We were also helped somewhat by some bad moves of our competitors. But to make a long story short, May was able to move up in the rankings and get its returns to the point where it was by far the most profitable company in the industry.

# REGINALD BRACK
**Chairman and CEO, Time Inc.**

When Reg Brack took over Time Inc. in 1989, the magazine giant ran on good-old-boy cronyism as much as anything else. It is no exaggeration to say that people expected to move up in the company because they were born into a prominent family, went to an Ivy League school, belonged to the right country club, or were involved in New York's high society.

Growth in the magazine business depends on the introduction of new products, a strong sense of consumer trends, smart editorial decisions, and attentiveness to advertising customers. Brack believed that if Time Inc. continued to rely on the culture of cronyism it had developed, it would dissolve into mediocrity. He needed to be certain that the company's growth would be led by the best people available in the field. Country club culture had no place in a modern, well-run media company.

———

WHEN I TOOK over Time Inc., it was well known for its old-boy network. I was the first non–Ivy Leaguer to ever head the company. I graduated from Washington & Lee. Cronyism was rampant. Before me, success depended much more on your golf handicap and who you knew than on your work skills and abilities. One result, and this is a shocking figure: at the corporate headquarters in 1986 we had no women in any position of authority higher than office manager.

The culture had to be changed—the most difficult thing a company can do—and it had to change to a performance orientation. Accomplishing this was my defining moment. At the time they're happening, you don't think of business decisions in terms of "moments," because changes come about naturally as the result of a process. However, the work we did to create our performance culture and our focus on customers stands apart.

I was aghast as I was coming up through the ranks at the way people were selected for jobs, and on several occasions I almost left the company because of it. There were people in key jobs I just could not respect.

I decided to get rid of the cronyism, and I put in a process by which any appointment had to be rigorously evaluated and a list of candidates of at least eight or ten had to be considered. The first major appointment of my tenure came when we had to replace the publisher of *Life* magazine. Several people came to me and said, "You know, I've been promised the next publisher's job," or, "So-and-so (one of my predecessors) promised me the job." I would say, "Okay, you're on the list, we'll see." We went ahead and used this new process. We ended up with our eight or ten candidates, met to discuss them, and ended up appointing a woman as publisher of *Life*. When we were leaving that meeting, my colleague said to me, "Reg, do you know what you just did?" I said, "What do you mean?" He said, "You just appointed the first female publisher of a Time Inc. magazine." I said, "Really? That wasn't even a consideration."

We went on to put women in key jobs because they were the best qualified for the job, not because we were trying to diversify. In fact, the chairman and CEO of Time Inc. today is a woman by the name of Ann Moore. I put her in her first real management position as publisher of *Sports Illustrated for Kids*.

Up until then, the company was a group of white males—WASPs. All of this changed as we moved to a performance orientation. I spent a number of years on the board of trustees of the National Urban League and was chairman of the board for four years. I learned more from the African American community about "diversity" than I could ever learn in seminars, and as a result, this helped me as we changed the culture at Time Inc. I was committed to getting people of color into the company to compete on merit along with everyone else. We're still not where we should be yet on this issue, but today people of color are in key jobs throughout Time Inc. The chairman and former CEO of the parent company, Time Warner, is Dick Parsons, probably one of the three most prominent African American executives today.

So instead of relying on cronyism, we instituted a fair process that would allow us to hire and promote the best candidates. When you change hiring and retention practices, you also have to be prepared for the other side of the coin, which is letting people go. That's the hardest thing I've ever had to do. Sometimes this is because their performance isn't cutting it, and sometimes because we had to make tough business choices that impacted jobs.

The only way I could sleep at night was to make absolutely certain that we were doing this in as compassionate a way as possible and providing as much of a safety net as we could. I had any number of people that were terminated come to me and say, "As bad as it was and as unhappy as I am, I have to say, it was done fairly and compassionately." And that's all you can hope for. It was always tough, because there were obviously hundreds and hundreds of people affected over time. In order to stay competitive and deliver the kind of results our shareholders and the Street demanded, we couldn't carry that kind of bloated cost structure that existed at the time.

Another aspect of the performance culture I was trying to establish was a focus on customers. I'm very proud of the fact that I'm the only CEO of the company who ever came up through sales and marketing. All of my predecessors, distinguished men that they were, came up either through journalism or, more likely than not, through finance. I had a sales orientation.

In those early years—that was the era of the three-martini lunch and pretty wild days, in fact there's literally been books written about the lifestyle of Time Inc. in those years—I made it a personal policy to stay away from the very people who were just having a good time. The products *Time* magazine and then *Sports Illustrated* and *Life* were so much in demand that it didn't take much to sell them. A good time was had by all. I just didn't operate that way and decided to spend as much time as humanly possible with the customers. I thought up all kinds of events: I took seventy-five people to see the first 747 roll out of a hangar. They were all customers from the airline industry and aviation. I took a similar group to Paris to see the Concorde fly for the first time. These were ways to put us in proximity with our clients at events they could never, ever arrange on their own. I concentrated on really taking good care of my customers and gave them experiences that would endear the company to them.

The new culture at Time Inc. meant high levels of performance. In that kind of environment, anybody who aspires to a management position or leadership position should focus on doing their job better than anybody has ever done it and not worry about the next job. Do your job better than anybody else has, learn what it takes for your boss to succeed, and make sure that she or he succeeds by the very nature of what you do. I was never focused on the next job. When I was running the book division, I never in a million years stopped and thought, *Well, if I do this well, they're going to make me head of magazines.* In fact, because of the cronyism at the time, I was sure they would not. I thought, *Well, I'll do the best I can here and we'll see. I guess I could go work someplace else.* But if you just focus on your job and on knowing what your manager expects, you're probably going to be okay.

# WILLIAM C. SWANEY
## President, Chairman, and CEO, Perrigo Company

---

Perrigo is the largest manufacturer of private-label vitamins and over-the-counter products in the country. It was a much smaller firm in 1978 when William Swaney was appointed president as the incumbent CEO's health began to fail. Perrigo's board of directors set one condition for Swaney's promotion: to prepare him for his leadership role, he had to take a course in executive management.

The course was a significant event in his evolution as a leader. It opened his eyes to the fact that Perrigo had no real professional management processes in place. Planning, budgeting, control, decision-making—the entire operation—were basically homegrown and ill suited for growth. He concluded that the company could be prepared for the future only through a complete overhaul of its management processes and a top-to-bottom transformation of its culture.

Perrigo was in a very competitive business. At the time there were many small vitamin and over-the-counter drug manufacturers calling on drugstores, supermarkets, and discount stores, all trying to develop them as long-term customers. These retailers were concerned about product selection, price, quality, and assurance of delivery in the quantities ordered. Many of them ran sales promotions of vitamins and over-the-counter products and counted on the reliability of their suppliers.

I know Bill Swaney and his company quite well. Perrigo was an important vendor for our company. When Swaney or one of his representatives told you something, you could believe it—you always knew where you stood. Bill himself had a reputation for integrity and reliability. He was a perfectionist who expected excellence from all the people who worked for him. Perrigo wasn't the cheapest source to buy from, but it was the best, and you didn't really mind paying more because you got what you paid for—superior quality, excellent packaging, and the quantities you needed when you needed them. Swaney's introduction of professional management really worked for Perrigo. In my opinion, they were the best in the business.

———

WHEN I ACCEPTED the position of president of the Perrigo Company in 1978, a board member insisted I take an AMA (American Management Association) course for presidents. He had been through the course and knew it would prepare me as an executive. The course really changed my whole perspective. I had no idea what it was really like to run a company. I'd been in manufacturing and sales before that.

The course was run by successful CEOs, and they taught the principles of professional management, which they built around planning, organization, and control. We had presentations by CEOs and consultants on those basic three modules. There was a great deal of attention on driving goal-setting and decision-making down to the lowest level possible—management by objectives, as it was called.

After this experience, I knew I had to change the management systems of our company from top to bottom. We had no formal or disciplined processes for management—virtually everything needed scrutiny and revision. In addition, we had to develop a culture that could accept and execute professional management.

I used the AMA program to do it. I wanted the company to run in a professionally managed way that would allow us to grow. I sent all my subordinates through the same course after I came back. As soon as each subordinate and department manager would come back, we would discuss what he learned and what I learned, and then we started implementing the professional management concept within each department. It took about a year to get it through the first level of management that reported to me. It took five years to get to the bottom—about a year for each level of management. Two major turnovers among my six or seven direct reports occurred as a result of their not liking the changes.

The concept we utilized is called the Unit President Concept. Every departmental manager in our company had the same set of responsibilities that I did as CEO. The only difference was scope. We taught a regular curriculum on this. At first we used the management course for presidents for the curriculum. That was for the first two or three years, but then we ended up developing our own. Anybody who joined us in a management capacity—and I don't care where they were in the company—they had to learn these concepts, and they had the same responsibilities that I did. The only difference was that they were responsible for a lesser dollar amount than I was. And these managers really took ownership.

The system not only allowed me to grow, it allowed everybody else involved in the company to grow. It was just so effective. The company was growing so fast, and we were able to have the decision-making process at the lowest possible level, where effective decisions could be made. We had a bunch of managers who were making big decisions that were two and three levels down from me. I want to tell you, it took a lot of stress off of growing the company.

The thing that was unique in this system at the time was that we controlled the business through standards of performance. We did that for two reasons: we tied the objectives in the plan to each one of the departments, and then that cascaded down into people's responsibilities. So in some way everyone had something to do with making our strategic plan, whether it was manufacturing, purchasing, or sales. But the most important thing was that we never used our performance standards for promotions or anything like that. We always used them for personal development. When we sat down with our managers, it was always a development tool. "What can we do better?" "What tools do we need to become more successful on the job?" It was kind of a unique way of appraising our employees back then, and it really was initiated by the employee. It was a self-appraisal system, and you just sat in and you critiqued it and then wrote a development plan as a result of that. It was very unique and effective at the time.

As part of our new culture, we really made a conscious effort to celebrate our successes. We worked hard to keep growing at 25 to 30 percent. In a manufacturing business, it's tough to keep that up. It takes a lot of effort. We would make our plans, and we'd have quarterly meetings; we would celebrate and acknowledge outstanding performance and pay a good quarterly bonus based on making the plan. Everybody in the company was on a bonus, all the hourly people as well as management.

When I went to change the culture of the company, I always used three key words: integrity, honesty, and respect. I wanted to build a company on integrity. I wanted our company to be honest with our customers and in our dealings with vendors. And I wanted everybody to have mutual respect for each other. Those were basically the three things I harped on at almost every meeting. Every meeting I used those three words. All of these changes put the business on the road to outstanding performance.

# CHAPTER 6

# The Mother of Invention: Transforming the Company's Business Model

The more things change, the more things . . . *continue to change.* When a large percentage of top business executives say the most important business decision they ever made was related to their effort to adapt the company to new circumstances, this tells me that managing change in an ever-changing business environment has got to be a core competency in any business.

If you looked at the speeches and writings from business leaders, politicians, academics, military leaders—you name it—from any period in history, they'll all at some point say, with complete conviction: "We are now in an unprecedented era of change." Regardless of the hyperbole, it is true that any leader needs to be ready, adaptable, and open-minded all the time because change is the constant.

One of the main drivers of change is technology. It's the factor most often cited as having accelerated the *pace* of change in our time. (So does that mean we really are in an unprecedented era of change?) New technologies are introducing disruptive forces into virtually every industry, and innovation cycles are getting much shorter. It's difficult enough keeping up with the gadgets used by middle-schoolers, but trying to integrate all of the latest advances in business technologies—communications, networking, database, Internet, and whatever else is "next gen"—is virtually impossible.

When you're scanning the horizon for change, however, you are looking at a variety of forces, not just technology. Globalization is no longer a buzzword of the future. It has washed over us completely, and competition now comes from every corner of the globe. Government has also taken a lead role. Policymakers and regulators have intervened to an extent that most of us never contemplated. Sometimes it's even difficult to tell friends from foes. Partners or vendors can quickly morph into competitors, and competitors can be turned into partners. It might be an exciting time to be in business, but it's also a nerve-wracking roller-coaster ride.

Sometimes change happens swiftly and dramatically. International events can have an impact on markets and industries quickly and without warning. In the wake of 9/11, the travel and hospitality industries were affected overnight, and it was years before they found their footing again. Even the economic crisis that began in 2008 seemed to come on pretty quickly. One quarter we were focused on growth, and the next quarter banks were going under and the dominos were falling.

Usually, however, we do have some foresight into oncoming changes—whether they are political, regulatory, economic, competitive, or consumer-driven. Even fast-paced technology developments rarely come without warning. The problem is usually not that we don't see them coming—it's that most industries take a while to digest the implications of change, and many of us tend to take a wait-and-see approach before reacting.

Look at the impact of the Internet on newspaper publishing. Many papers are fighting for their lives because of the changing way readers get their news and the changing way advertisers reach their audiences. The shift of both to the Internet did not happen overnight. The print media had plenty of opportunity to see this trend coming, yet they are now desperately trying to find a business model that works.

Often people are acutely aware of the changing conditions around them (let's give the buggy whip makers some credit—I'm sure they saw it coming), but they nevertheless simply try to hang on as long as possible because either they are not equipped to capitalize on the new circumstances or they hope there is enough market left over after the wave of change has passed over them.

Not all changes are dramatic, but every company faces the same basic challenge: how to react to a changing business environment. Sometimes the right response comes from visionary leaders and gut instinct. But for those of us who aren't soothsayers, more often it comes through the disciplined management practice of planning, anticipating, and adjusting.

I used to put our company through a rigorous planning process that started with an analysis of our industry and the effects of external forces. For example, in the drugstore business it wasn't always the case that supermarkets and discount stores carried a lot of the same products as our drugstores. But we slowly began to see more and more shelf space in those other sectors dedicated to health and beauty products, household items, school supplies, and so on. Then the supermarkets and discount stores started opening pharmacies inside their stores—that was a shot across the bow of our highest-margin products. At the same time, large health care insurers began to cap the reimbursement for prescriptions.

These were all big challenges in our business, but they are typical of what every company and every industry experiences. Whatever the external factors are—competitors, regulatory changes, consumer behavior trends, price pressure, technological innovations—they must be tracked closely and analyzed for their impact or potential impact.

Once the external trends and forces were identified, we would map our strategy to the business environment. This was used to drive a very detailed one-year plan and a less detailed five-year plan. Nothing was sacred. Changes were welcome if they made sense. (A useful tool for this type of analysis is described in the next chapter.)

We then drilled down into every aspect of the business—we had a sales and marketing plan, a logistics plan, a human resource plan, a technology plan, a physical assets plan, a financial plan. For each plan, we'd examine ways to improve, evaluate whether our assumptions were realistic, and make sure the different plans complemented each other.

When a company finds that it is underperforming, it is tempting to look at draconian measures—cutting costs across the board, dropping underperforming product lines, focusing on core assets. What the planning process enables is a response that zeros in on the problems. Sometimes a large-scale response (layoffs, cost-cutting, selling underperforming businesses) is the answer, but sometimes it's not; it's important for your business that you respond to the actual problem.

The sexy stuff of business is generally not found in the nuts and bolts of a detailed management and planning process. We'd all rather be out there selling, marketing, expanding, and doing deals. But I found this type of process to be crucial, not because I wanted the company to follow any given plan to the letter, but because it gave us a foundation for knowing where we were going and how we would get there. I never had a problem reevaluating strategy, going off budget, or changing tactics, but I always wanted a compelling reason for doing it. If it made sense, we'd revise the plan and move on. Whether a change was big or small, proactive or reactive, it didn't matter. I wanted to run the analysis, revise the plans, and build a conceptual foundation before managing through the change.

Every business goes through some kind of dramatic change at

some point. No one stagnates their way to greatness. Even the market leaders must adapt, innovate, and take chances. Perhaps we more often see big changes from companies as a defensive tactic, but some change their strategies or models proactively to move up in the pack or keep themselves in front of the pack. These are the real innovators.

The changes that the executives in this chapter implemented did not come easy. Even when responding to declining performance, human inertia is a powerful physical force in business. As we'll see in these stories, the law of human inertia is in constant tension with the more formidable law of perpetual environmental motion—every aspect of the business environment is constantly changing. Great management is indeed about managing change.

## SHELLY LAZARUS
**Chairman and CEO, Ogilvy & Mather Worldwide**

S helly Lazarus describes herself as passionate. She is certainly passionate about her work and her family. She would like to be remembered as someone who had a successful career and a successful marriage and who was able to be a good mother without sacrificing anything of importance in her business or family life.

Most objective observers would agree that she has accomplished all of these goals and then some: she has a happy, long-lasting marriage and a fine family, and in her career she rose to the pinnacle of the advertising world as head of Ogilvy & Mather Worldwide.

As you will read in the following story, Lazarus sees in her career three key decisions that worked together to add to her own accomplishments and at the same time move Ogilvy toward a new model of service for its clients.

Lazarus is fond of quoting David Ogilvy, one of the most famous ad men who ever lived and a cofounder of her firm: "If we hire people who are larger than we are, we will become a company of giants. If we hire people who are smaller than we are, we will become a company of midgets." In Shelly Lazarus, Ogilvy most certainly found one of his giants.

Lazarus has served as president of Ogilvy Direct and Ogilvy North America, among other executive positions. She was named CEO of Ogilvy & Mather Worldwide in 1996 and added the title of chairman in 1997. Lazarus relinquished the title of CEO in 2008 and remains chairman of the firm.

———

THERE HAVE BEEN several key moments in my career.

The first was a personal decision to go back to work after I had a third child.

The second, from a company point of view, was when I made the decision to run Ogilvy Direct, the direct-marketing arm of our firm. I volunteered to go and run it at a time when it was looked at as sort of a poor sister by the rest of Ogilvy. It didn't have the status that advertising had. In a way, it was thought of as just being about "junk mail."

Another critical decision occurred in 1996 when I was asked to come back and run the advertising agency four years after I left to run Ogilvy Direct. We had been acquired by WWP Group, an English company, in a hostile takeover, and now the advertising agency was completely falling apart. The takeover had been a traumatic event for the company, as it is for any company. The new owners had gone through three different CEOs, and the company was a mess, with terrible tension between the acquirers and the people in the agency.

The easy decision for me would have been to just stay over at Ogilvy Direct, where things were going swimmingly and I wouldn't have to deal with all this turmoil. But at the end of the day, I thought, if these guys in the ad agency didn't survive, then Ogilvy Direct wasn't going to survive either. So I went.

In a way, these moments worked together. People thought I was nuts to go to Ogilvy Direct, and yet I saw that it had enormous promise if you put the disciplines together. It wasn't that direct marketing wasn't interesting in and of itself—it was. But what was really interesting to me was to do direct marketing and advertising hand in hand for a single client. I saw that putting them together would have tremendous benefits for our clients and their brands.

That, plus other disciplines we went into beyond advertising, really became the foundation for what we now call "360 degree brand stewardship." We put all the disciplines together, and that allowed us to create a whole strategy for a company and integrate a single communications plan for a client.

Ogilvy Direct, which is now called Ogilvy One, grew organically in the company. We took some people and planted them in a place and said, "Start doing the direct marketing for American Express." With some acquisitions along the way, it grew to be the largest direct-response company in the world.

We went into public relations, and again, that was a combination of some acquisitions and also moving people to different places and telling them to start a PR agency and grow it.

In addition, we grew by acquisitions outside the United States, because the real imperative was to be able to manage global brands for global clients, which meant that we had to be present in markets all over the world.

I don't think I could have accomplished what I have if I weren't passionate about what I do. If you don't like what you do, you're not going to be successful at it, I don't care how hard you try.

I also like to have a little fun. I tell people—you spend an enormous amount of time in your professional life, and it's okay to sit back and just smile and laugh once in a while. Otherwise, the tension will eat you up. As CEO, I've tried to create an environment where people can put their feet up on your table and sit back and just laugh. I can tell you, it works.

## LESTER SHERMAN
**President, Wohl Shoe Company**

L ester Sherman loves the shoe business and has spent his entire career there. In fact, he started selling shoes at the age of thirteen. Now in his eighties, he is still involved, helping out at his son's discount shoe store.

His passion for the business took the form of a lifelong career with the Wohl Shoe Company. Sherman rose to the position of president and successfully guided the company through some of its rockiest moments. During his years there, the number of Wohl shoe outlets more than doubled.

Wohl sold shoes through a variety of outlets, but its core business was leasing space and setting up shoe departments in department stores all over the country. Macy's and Dayton Hudson were just two of the many department stores Wohl worked with.

Sherman's defining moment arrived uninvited, when a devastating threat suddenly emerged. Through no fault of his own or his company's, he was about to lose a huge piece of business— approximately $110 million in sales. His quick and definitive response spearheaded a transformation in the way Wohl did business and sold its shoes. And it saved the company.

The Wohl name no longer exists, but the fruit of Sherman's work lives on as the billion-dollar business of the Brown Shoe Company.

I STARTED SELLING shoes at the age of thirteen, and I worked for Wohl Shoe Company for thirty-three years. Of course, my defining moment took place in the shoe business.

The company I worked for most of my life was started by David P. Wohl. He came up with the concept of leasing space in women's specialty stores, and eventually that evolved into leasing space in department stores. The concept of lease departments and selling our shoes out of them was really the core of Wohl Shoe Company's business, and it was a very successful concept.

We leased in department stores all over the country: Macy's, Dayton Hudson, Foley's, Carson Perry Scott, May Company—and I could keep on naming them because we were in department stores in almost every major city in the country. We sold women's, men's, and children's shoes.

I became president of Wohl on March 5, 1981, and after being president for just six months, I was informed that Macy's stores throughout the country were going to take over their own shoe business and that we had to be out of their stores in one year. At the time we were doing around $110 million a year in Macy's. We had Macy's in New York, in Atlanta, in Kansas City, and out in California. We had been a lessee of Macy's for twenty-two years.

Prior to their announcement, I had been assured in person by the president of Macy's that they were very pleased with our partnership and were looking forward to the future with us. We felt very secure with them. When I became president, I had made a trip to New York City and attended a charitable dinner at a cost of $5,000 a plate. It was a black-tie affair at the 21 Club in New York, and I sat at the table with the president of Macy's. After the dinner, he put his arm around me and assured me how happy they were with Wohl Shoe Company's operation. And then six months later they canceled our leases.

The reason, to my knowledge, was that we operated the shoe business in Foley's department store in Houston, Texas, and it was a very big business. It was the number-one department store and one of our largest shoe volume departments. Macy's decided to go into Houston. But because of our prior association with Foley's, we had to decline going with Macy's and setting up a shoe department in their Houston store. To my knowledge, that's the reason they canceled us—not because we weren't doing well, but because they didn't like the fact that we would not be able to work with them when they opened up in Houston. So they canceled and they gave us one year's notice.

Now I was faced with trying to regain $110 million in sales very quickly. What I decided to do was the biggest decision I ever made, and it became my defining moment.

We had just bought a company called Famous Footwear. They had thirty stores, and they were doing $30 million, so that's an average of a million dollars a store. I figured that if we could get Famous Footwear up to 110 stores, and if we were successful, I could make up all of the Macy's volume. We set up a new division in St. Louis, in addition to the division Famous already had in Madison, Wisconsin, which is where the company was founded. St. Louis was going to open stores in the southern portion of the United States, and Madison was going to expand in the northern half of the United States.

We moved very quickly and proceeded to open up about fifty stores a year. When I left Wohl five years later, we had over three hundred stores, and we had made up all of Macy's volume and then some. Today Famous Footwear is doing over $1.2 billion in sales a year.

That decision to move quickly into our own stores instead of staying with leased shoe departments was a major change in direction for Wohl's business model. I think it still would have happened if we hadn't lost Macy's, but it would have been a much, much slower process.

In some ways it was an easy decision, so I won't take a lot of credit for it. I was kind of pushed into it. Losing Macy's business was personally a big emotional blow as well as a financial blow for my company. In fact, it was the most emotional thing I've ever been through at Wohl's. Reacting to the problem on a business level, though, wasn't the emotional part—I found that challenging.

The Famous Footwear concept was a big risk. If it was not successful, it could have been devastating for the company and for me. If it hadn't worked, I wouldn't have been in that job for very long.

When I started with Wohl in 1953, we had about 1,000 leased shoe departments. By the time I retired, we had approximately 2,200 operations, including freestanding stores, mall stores, and, of course, the leased shoe departments. Famous Footwear was a major part of our growth.

I'm retired now, but I work as a volunteer in a large discount shoe store that my son owns. I still love the shoe business.


## ALBERT E. SUTER

**Vice Chairman and COO, Emerson Electric Company;
President, Whirlpool Corporation; President,
Firestone Corporation**

---

Albert Suter has run some big corporations, including Whirlpool and Firestone, and he spent many years at a distinguished management consulting firm. But when asked to discuss the most important decision of his career, Suter chose to talk about his time at Emerson Electric.

Emerson Electric Company is one of the best-managed businesses in America. Its management style is tough, professional, and focused on achieving consistently high profits.

As a senior manager at Emerson, Suter was governed by a realistic and disciplined planning and execution process that always found ways to cut costs, develop more efficient processes, and buy better and smarter.

Suter's tenure at Emerson took place at the dawn of globalization in the early 1980s. The problem he and Emerson faced back then is still a problem as fresh as today's headlines: foreign producers were crippling one of his businesses by making and selling a high-quality product at a much lower price.

Emerson was losing business and losing market share. But cutting prices would have destroyed its margins and swept away the hope of high future profits. Suter helped Emerson chart its course out of a disastrous situation and back to a leadership position in its markets.

The actions taken by Suter and his company were a harbinger of a movement that would be joined by many U.S. companies over the next three decades. What they did remains controversial—the subject of bitter public and political debate—and has had lasting ramifications for the health of American companies and American workers.

Emerson has grown into a global manufacturing and technology company with $25 billion in sales. It employs more than 140,000 people in 265 manufacturing locations worldwide.

———

THE PIVOTAL POINT in my career came as globalization was hitting us here in the States. These were the very early years of globalization. The toughest challenge we had at Emerson during that time—and I think all U.S. industries—was when we started to find out that we had very tough offshore competition.

For years the Japanese were selling into the United States, but people said their products were poor quality, that they were just taking the low-end markets. I remember one meeting when we realized that we were not growing as fast as our markets were growing. Yet, when you talked to all of our divisions, which we did every year when they gave us a five-year plan, no one was losing share. If no one is losing share, how can we be growing slower than the market?

Well, then we found out that several divisions at Emerson were saying, "Well, the Japanese came into the low end, and we lost that, but we don't consider that part of our market anymore." They just kept redefining the market. In reaction, we passed the rule that the market is the market, not only in the United States but globally, and we wanted to start talking about *global* share. That's when we started realizing we were losing share to imports.

The next revelation was a big one: we lost a big chunk of business from Whirlpool. They were an important customer and were buying motors from us that they used in their refrigerator compressors.

Whirlpool figured a compressor was costing them over $40 a unit. At the same time, the U.S. government had passed new energy efficiency laws for refrigerator compressors, and they had to spend millions of dollars to redesign the product and retool their plant.

It happened that Whirlpool owned a portion of Brastemp, a Brazilian appliance company. Brastemp made refrigerators and made their own compressors at a separate compressor company called Embraco.

Embraco offered to sell Whirlpool compressors that would meet the new energy efficiency standards for under $30 a unit—a significantly lower price. Whirlpool thought that made sense, especially since they owned part of Brastemp. They shut down their compressor plant and started buying all of their compressors from

Embraco. We had also been selling the motors to a company called Tecumseh, who made compressors for Whirlpool. Between the two of those, we were losing our two largest customers. We were losing something between $300 and $350 million in sales out of a total business of $500 million.

With that kind of loss, we just couldn't stay in that business anymore. In essence we had lost the entire $500 million business in these motors.

We had to find out what was going on. We all thought that maybe Brazil was subsidizing this motor compressor manufacturing. So I went down to Brazil and visited the plant and looked at their operations, and they showed us all the numbers. There were some government subsidies—agreed—but the government subsidies just offset the higher duties they had to pay to bring in equipment and bring in copper from Chile. And when we looked at their process and the design of the compressor, it turned out to be better than the U.S. efficiency standard.

They had equipped the plant down there with production equipment as good as any in the world. They got equipment from Germany, Italy, Switzerland, and their processes were as productive as ours and produced a quality product.

When we went down there, we kind of expected to find a bunch of unsophisticated businesspeople. When I got off the airplane and the guy started speaking Portuguese, I said, "I'm sorry, I don't speak Portuguese. I only speak English and German." So they switched to German—perfect German. They took me to the plant the next day and showed me a plant as modern as anything we had in this country. Their cost structure was such that they had equal or slightly better material and labor content than ours. However, they were paying hourly people a dollar an hour and paying engineers $12,000 a year. They were also sourcing component parts from local manufacturers who had the same cost structure. In the U.S.

back then, we were paying labor at least $15 an hour and paying engineers $40,000 to $50,000 a year. When you put all the numbers together, they could sell that compressor to companies in the United States for less than $30 a unit and make decent profit. Ten dollars less than we could.

Their cost structure was much lower than ours, and it turned out that their quality standards were as good as or better than ours. In Brazil they weren't even worried about meeting our U.S. quality standards. One of their guys said to me, "We have to meet the quality challenges of the world."

I sort of jumped out and said, "You mean our quality levels?!"

He said, "No, no, no. The United States doesn't count. You guys are nowhere near the quality of the Japanese. They are the ones who count!"

In the U.S. we were still talking about rejected parts in full percents. If you had 99 percent good product with 1 percent rejects, you were in great shape. Well, the Japanese talked parts per million—tenths or hundredths of a percent of rejects.

When I got back from Brazil and reported back to the company, I said, "These guys are for real. This isn't about government subsidies. These guys are for real." We sat down at Emerson and said, "Okay, we've lost this business, but we can't lose any more. We have to find a way to become cost-competitive with these companies around the world."

Our realization was that the competition was not just other U.S. manufacturers—we were competing with all of these emerging countries on a global basis. We realized that over time we would have to lower prices to meet this competition, and then we'd say, "Okay, we've got to figure out how to take that price decrease and still make money."

That's when we made the most important decision in the history of our company: we had to move our production to global areas that had the same cost structure as our new emerging competition. That was the only way we could lower our prices and survive.

We set up a "best cost producer" program at Emerson to ensure that we would become globally competitive. If we had to move half the jobs in a plant to Mexico or China, we had no choice. It was either that or lose the entire business.

We started this in the early 1980s, when we had about 5 percent of our jobs in low-cost countries, and now we're up to 65 percent in low-cost areas.

These events culminated when I and the other top management decided we had to move jobs offshore. We started first with moving jobs to best-cost areas and then started sourcing material in these same areas, as we found we could get the same quality materials at lower cost. Over the years we continued to move more offshore. It wasn't the desired strategy. Of course not. But it was basically a realization and commitment that we were going to do what we needed to do in order to save the business.

A newspaper got hold of this and criticized Emerson's CEO in an article. At the time he made the statement, "We moved jobs to save jobs." His point was that in the compressor motor business, we lost the whole business: not only hourly workers, but we lost supervisors, salespeople, and the engineers. So we made the decision that from now on we were going to lose some hourly jobs in order to save the rest of the jobs.

Deciding to make this happen was the critical moment for me. We started forcing the issue with our managers, saying, "Tell us what your competitor's cost is. Now, at that cost structure, what price can he afford? Now, how are you going to meet that price?" Unfortunately, nine times out of ten the answer is moving jobs and material sourcing to best-cost global areas.

# JOHN F. MCDONNELL
## Chairman and CEO, McDonnell Douglas Corporation

S ome business decisions take a tremendous emotional toll. Perhaps the toughest ones are when a company decides it must reduce its workforce. No CEO takes such an action lightly, and he or she must carry the burden of a decision that affects the lives of employees and their families.

John McDonnell, the gentlemanly, mild-mannered chairman of McDonnell Douglas, knows this all too well. First he had to solve management problems at the company's Douglas Aircraft division, which had run into trouble. He ended up replacing top management and putting in a whole new management structure.

Next, he had to solve the tremendous cost problems that were bleeding his company dry. McDonnell attacked that problem on two fronts. One, already mentioned, was to reduce the workforce and drastically cut expenses and investments. The second was to change the way his company did business with the federal government, forcing a move from fixed-price to "cost-plus" development contracts.

McDonnell not only brought his company back to life but also changed the way the industry conducted business.

McDonnell was named CEO in 1988 and served in that capacity until September 1994. He continued to serve as chairman of McDonnell Douglas until 1997, when it merged with Boeing. McDonnell is currently a member of the board of directors of Boeing.

———

IN 1939 MY father started McDonnell Aircraft. During World War II, it basically did subcontract work for other aircraft companies like Boeing and Douglas. Then, right at the end of World War II, it got its first prime contract. That was for the original Phantom, which was the first all jet carrier–based fighter plane. Other contracts followed.

I started full-time with the company in 1962 after I got my master's degree in aeronautical engineering. My first assignment was working on the Gemini spacecraft.

In 1967 the company merged with Douglas Aircraft and became McDonnell Douglas Corporation. Douglas was more than double the size of McDonnell, and the merged company became one of the largest aircraft companies in the world. In 1966, the year before the merger with Douglas, our revenue was just over $1 billion. After, in 1967, it went to just under $3 billion.

An important part of the story is told in the number of people employed by the combined company. In 1962, when I joined McDonnell, we had 23,900 full-time employees; when I retired, it was 63,900. In between, at our peak, we had over 135,000 employees—that was in 1990.

Between 1990 and 1993, we reduced the number of employees by half, from 135,000 to about 65,000. That was the hardest thing I ever had to do. To turn the company around I had to institute and implement "hard reality" at McDonnell Douglas.

We were in a position where we had to dramatically reduce our costs, lay off people, and change the way we did business. It was that dire. The cause was that a commercial airliner development program and three major military aircraft development programs were all based on fixed-price contracts, and they were all hemorrhaging cash. Concurrently, there was an economic recession causing banks to drastically curtail new lending, so we had to eliminate our cash outflow in order to survive. Making that decision, with all of its ramifications, and deciding how we would go about it and what we were and were not willing to sacrifice were all necessary to position us to survive and be able to thrive in the future.

When we decided that drastic action must be taken, obviously all the employees in the company felt very vulnerable. The way we handled that was to try to communicate as much as possible about what we were doing and why. Here, for example, is a letter I issued throughout the company in July 1990:

Our Cost Reduction Plan

Today I am announcing a corporate-wide plan to reduce annual costs by more than $700,000,000. The major elements of the plan are as follows: reduce our workforce, including contract hires by 14,000 to 17,000 people by the end of the year; continue with our stringent capital budget cutbacks; make significant cuts in budgets for travel, consultants, advertising, and other support activities; cut the amount of overtime, and greatly restrict overtime payments to most salaried exempt people; temporarily cut in half company contributions to the salaried savings plan. This will be reviewed for restoration at the end of 1991, or sooner if financial conditions warrant.

I deeply regret the pain and hardship that the job cuts will cause thousands of people who have been valued and dedicated employees of the corporation. Assistance will be provided to help these people find new jobs and opportunities. In most locations, this will include such things as job fairs, résumé services, and counseling.

In recent months I have told you about our unsatisfactory financial performance and the magnitude of our challenges. Still, I am sure that many of you are wondering: Why? Why is it necessary to put thousands of people out of work? The immediate answer is that we must demonstrate that we are taking aggressive action to improve our financial performance. . . . In the longer term we must reduce costs to be profitable in our highly competitive and rapidly changing marketplace. This applies to both our government and commercial businesses.

I accept responsibility for the fact that we must take these harsh actions now. In retrospect, it is clear that we made some mistakes in the course of our reorganizations. We did not do enough to establish the boundaries that would prevent excessive duplication of functions and services, and we did not exercise sufficient control over costs and staffing. It took us too long to recognize that we had too many people on the payroll. In fact we did everything but face the issue of layoffs. We cut costs, we trimmed expenses, we started selling off some of our businesses and commercial real estate, and we kept hoping for increased profitability. A direct pay cut would not be a long-term solution because we would risk losing critical skills. That leaves us with the hard reality of significant layoffs.

Deep as they are, I believe that we can make these cuts so that they will not jeopardize our technological capability or undermine our ability to deliver quality products on time. . . .

That cutback and subsequent ones in the next three years resulted in reducing our total employment from about 135,000 people to about 65,000 people, closing a number of large facilities, selling several businesses, cutting capital expenditures by more than 80 percent, reducing travel by one-half, slashing overhead, and cutting our dividend in half. Each time we instigated a new round of cutbacks, our remaining team rose to the challenge and developed better ways to get the necessary work done.

By taking all those drastic actions, we not only survived, but we were better positioned for the future. Within a year, the aerospace market, both commercial and military, started declining. As a result, we were ahead of our competitors in terms of restructuring ourselves for that environment. Within three years, we were a very strong competitor. Throughout that trying time, we did not cut back research and development (R&D), and we did not reduce our employee training or our coverage of employees' expenses for all educational courses, because we believed that having a highly educated, motivated workforce and a robust R&D program were essential for our future. Those were expenses we consciously decided not to cut back while we were significantly cutting back everything else.

At the end of the three-year period, we had reduced our debt from over $3 billion to under $1.5 billion. We were achieving record earnings. Our stock price was at an all-time high of well over $100 per share, compared to the low $30s at the time the "hard reality" decision was made.

One very simple lesson from all of this, for the entire aerospace business, was—don't enter into fixed-price development contracts. Major aerospace defense programs are so complex and technologically challenging that the contractor and customer must work very closely together. A fixed-price environment prevents that from happening. From that searing experience we, the whole aerospace industry, and the government customer learned that lesson and changed the form of major development contracts to cost plus incentive fee. If I had not faced up to all of our problems, the company may not have gone out of business, but it certainly would not have been in a position to merge with Boeing in 1997 at an equivalent price of more than $450 per share.

Another lesson I learned was that costs can be reduced from "business as usual" much more than it is possible to analytically predict at the outset. During the three-year period, we had three rounds of cost-cutting, each of which represented at least a 10 percent reduction, and each of which was considered highly risky. Yet at the end of the period the company was still designing, developing, and building quality products.

It turned out that all the changes we made not only were necessary to restore our strength but also prepared us for what turned out to be an industry-changing period of corporate consolidations in the mid-1990s.

## JAMES NIXON
**President, Whitman's Chocolate Company**

J im Nixon is a hardworking, loyal, solid individual. When he tells you something, you can bank on it. Nixon always gave his company his maximum effort. Even when asked to move his family around the country ten or so times as he rose through the ranks at Pet, Inc., he did it with enthusiasm. Eventually, he was able to settle down in Philadelphia when he took the reins at Whitman's Chocolate Company, a Pet subsidiary.

Nixon became something of a corporate problem-solver for Pet, and a man the company knew it could rely on in a pinch. When a company expands and diversifies quickly, as Pet did, it can find itself facing problems—and opportunities—that are outside its comfort zone. That's when Nixon would be sent in.

When he took over at Whitman's, Nixon immediately saw the need for change. The company was losing money, and it needed to overhaul its operations, modernize its management, and revitalize its approach to marketing. Plus, it was overstaffed.

Nixon put his stamp on the company in a big way, turning it around and restoring it to long-term profitability.

Throughout his career, Nixon's only interest was doing what was in the best interest of Pet. I worked at Pet at the same time as Jim. I was running a chain of retail drugstores and pharmacies, and we competed with a number of drugstore chains that also happened to be important customers of Whitman's. Some of these drug chains complained to top management at Pet about us. Some even indicated that they would stop buying and stocking Whitman's candy in retaliation.

As head of Whitman's, Nixon could easily have joined the chorus of complaints or tried in some way to make us responsive to his customers' concerns. After all, their defection would have hurt his sales. Instead, he sided with us, believing that the company as a whole benefited from our work in a way that outweighed the potential loss of sales in his Whitman's division. Not many executives would have acted as Jim did. It's a tribute to his character. And incidentally, he never did lose any of those sales.

---

I WORKED FOR Pet in many different jobs and in many parts of the country, starting as a retail salesman in the Philadelphia area selling Pet evaporated milk. When I first joined the company, it was basically a one-product company, and I helped build the business through their infant-feeding markets.

There were certainly some turbulent years at Pet. The company foresaw that the evaporated milk business would decline. Since it was their only major business, they realized they'd better diversify. So in 1956 they started a program of acquisitions, buying some fourteen companies over the next several years, all related, directly or indirectly, to the food business or the drug business. Eventually Pet amassed a diverse collection of businesses in food, food storage, retail drug, liquor, restaurant, and other industries.

I became involved in a lot of these different businesses, including diet foods and grocery products. We ended up moving around a lot: Washington, Buffalo, St. Louis, Detroit, San Francisco. And I was often on the road no matter where we happened to live.

Nobody ever said to me, "You have to take this assignment and move." It was always, "Look, there's an opportunity, and we think you can fill the job, and we'd like you to take it." The inference, though, and it was pretty true throughout industry in those days, was that if you were ever going to get anywhere in a company, you had to agree to move when the opportunity presented itself. The rule of thumb used to be that if you turned down two moves, you could figure you were going to stay in your current job for the rest of your life. Invariably, if they were going to advance you, the advancement opportunity came in some other part of the country and you had to move.

The position of vice president of marketing at the Whitman's Chocolate division opened up, and they asked me if I would be interested in that. I had *no* interest in moving back to Philadelphia, but this offer seemed like something we could be very happy with. I was familiar with Whitman's. It had a good reputation in the industry. It had a good reputation in Philadelphia and was recognized as one of the quality companies in the area.

So we agreed to move back to Philadelphia. This was in 1969, and I took over as vice president of marketing. A year later the chap who was president of Whitman's retired and was replaced by another gentleman. After a year he left the company and I was appointed general manager to run the Whitman's Chocolate division. A year and a half later they formally appointed me president. From that point on, from 1971 until 1987, when I retired, I was president of Whitman's Chocolate.

The event that most shaped me as a businessman came when I took over as president. Whitman's was struggling, and I took a hard look at the entire business. I had my work cut out for me. Whitman's had been on the decline for several consecutive years: sales were down and earnings were down. They really were experiencing some difficult financial problems.

The first thing we did was look at the cost structure. They were overstaffed, which was one thing that was rather obvious. They had about a third more people than they needed to run the business. We made some drastic cuts in personnel right off and changed some of the other operating procedures. We were able to change things around the first year to where we stabilized the earnings drop. From that time on, until I retired in 1987, our sales and earnings were up every year.

Then we looked at marketing. We brought in some new people, and we did it over a period of time. But right from the start, we gave it direction that it obviously lacked. There was really nobody hitting the marketing area. There was an old-line sales manager. He'd been there for years, knew a lot of the customers, and was operating the same way he had operated twenty years before. And he was difficult to get along with.

One of the keys to the turnaround: we set up a new environment, one that stressed participatory management. Of course, we saw people on a day-to-day basis, but we also held mandatory monthly staff meetings where everyone's input was heard. We looked at where we were going, how we were doing with the plans we had made for the year. We had everybody sitting around the same table. There were eight men who reported to me directly, and we saw to it that each of them participated. If they didn't join in, they knew they would be called on. We would go around the table and say, "Okay, we want to hear from each of you. What are your problems? Where do you see opportunity?" We had participation of the whole group of top people in the company, and the anchor for this was our monthly meetings. We had input from everyone, and everyone was accountable to each other. It wasn't always comfortable but it worked.

In terms of revenue, we were about $700,000 when I joined the company, then on down to $650,000 the year I took over. Over the course of my tenure, we grew sales into the $5 million to $6 million range, and we became quite profitable.

I liked the success—I can't deny that. If the company had continued to go down, my star would have fallen along with it. I have to say, when you see success from things that you've done, things you initiated, and you see them over a lengthy period of time, not just one year—that just gives you a good, warm, and proud feeling.

## LLOYD SCHERMER
### President, CEO, and Chairman, Lee Enterprises

The newspaper business is in crisis as it tries to adjust to the impact of digital media and the changing ways people get their news and information. Newspapers are now making a difficult transition into a hybrid of print and online media. While print circulation is down, studies show total readership of print coupled with newspaper websites is growing. Yet layoffs, pay cuts, and bankruptcies have become commonplace in the industry, and several papers, often number-two players in their markets, have folded, including the *Seattle Post-Intelligencer*, the *Rocky Mountain News*, and the *Madison Capital Times*. Others, such as the venerable *Christian Science Monitor*, have left the print world behind and now exist only online.

This is not the first time that technology and print journalism have collided. In 1954, when Lloyd Schermer joined the large newspaper chain Lee Enterprises, one of his first jobs, as he will tell you, was as a scab—a strikebreaker. The company was trying to automate in order to increase productivity and remain profitable. The union opposed the moves with a strike. The new composing systems that Lee wanted to put in place would dramatically increase the speed of typesetting and require less skill than the old equipment. But it would also cost some people their jobs.

During this period, Schermer did every job, from setting type to working the presses. He would get so dirty that on his return home from work his wife would make him take his clothes off out on the porch so she could clean them or burn them.

Schermer rose to the position of president and CEO of Lee Enterprises in 1973. He led the company firmly but compassionately through another difficult and wrenching period of modernization, which included massive layoffs as well as a revolution in its corporate governance. As a leader, he knew where he had to take the company, and he didn't hesitate.

Lee owns forty-nine daily newspapers, rapidly growing online news sites, and three hundred other publications in twenty-three states.

———

When I took over at Lee Enterprises, I knew it was a big job and was going to be difficult. It was a big step for me to run the whole damn thing. But it didn't scare me. I'd been in many leadership roles, and I was ready.

Socrates said, "Know thyself," and I think I understood myself. That's where it starts. It's important, especially for young people: if they want to get ahead in the world, they have to try to begin to understand themselves, where they're coming from, what motivates them, and how they can motivate and lead other people. Learning about yourself and how your behaviors influence other people is extraordinarily important.

Not everybody can be a leader—but in my own career, leadership is exactly where I've concentrated my efforts. It's always fascinated me, and it's been my consuming interest. A lot of my understanding came from what I saw this country do for my father, for a lot of the immigrants in Granite City, Illinois, where I grew up. My dad was a Hungarian immigrant. He came over in the early 1900s with his six brothers, and they settled in Granite City, Illinois. It was a town of immigrants—a steel town.

These people spent most of their lives at work—not at home, but in the work environment. This is where their sustenance came from. I saw this when I was very young and would wonder about how you motivate those people in their work. That's where leadership comes in.

I learned that you can't force people to change or to do things they don't want to do. As a leader, you've got to open the door to opportunity, and they have to take it. You can't spoon-feed it. You open the door, and the ones who really want it, they'll walk right through the door and grab it.

So with all my experience and my ideas about leading, I was ready to take up the challenge to lead Lee Enterprises.

I knew I was facing a lot of tough decisions. One of them was deciding what to do with a third of all of our production forces who would have to be laid off when we converted our composing rooms from hot metal typesetting to cold type—a photographic process. We were not about to give guaranteed lifetime jobs in this changeover. That does not help people with their dignity, and it doesn't help the company. But on the other hand, when you lay people off, you're destroying the livelihoods of a lot of families.

Convincing our publishers in their heads that it had to be done for the sake of the business—that was easy. But convincing them in their hearts—that was very difficult. These were communities we were dealing with—people out in Montana, for example, at the *Billings Gazette*. Everyone goes to the same church; their kids go to the same schools; they all grew up together. They're all part of the community. When you're in management and you've got to lay people off, you still have to live with them.

We had to win their minds and their hearts, but that was extremely hard to do. You have to win over the confidence of people so they believe what you say. And then you have to do what you say you're going to do and not play games with them. You tell them the truth, you tell them that their jobs are going to become obsolete, but that we'll help them learn a new job.

We put together some very innovative ways of helping people maintain a means of livelihood. We eventually won over the unions in our company with the programs we put in place, so that over a period of fifteen years sixty bargaining units decertified voluntarily and Lee became a non-union company, and many of our key positions became occupied by ex-union people—publishers and so forth.

One of the most innovative things we did was to help some guys get franchises. The union president in Missoula, Montana, bought an AAMCO Transmissions franchise. We helped him get it and he started a whole new business. We helped some people go to another employer. We subsidized them on the job with their new employer until they learned the new skills, and we retrained a lot of people in all parts of the company.

The other big issue I knew I was going to face when I became CEO was the board of directors.

You know, Washington can pass all the statutes they want, and companies can write all kinds of job specs, and it doesn't mean a thing. What you need are people who have leadership skills who are confident in their own ability and they're willing to be put under the microscope and be inspected by independent directors who are under no pressure except to say what they really believe. It comes down to having a CEO who has enough confidence in himself or herself so they don't have to put their friends on the board but will instead go with outsiders who know their stuff.

I wanted an independent board, and even before I became CEO, we put a fellow named Dave Jaquith on, whom I had met through the American Management Association. He had a reputation for being a tough and disciplined businessman, and I knew he'd be good for the company. I told my boss, "If we get him, our lives will never be the same, because he is a true independent director. Believe me, it's gonna be different." And once he became a director, things did begin to change—we started getting good, objective advice on issues we were facing and honest criticism of some of our actions.

Within eight or nine months of my becoming CEO, the board decided to go back to quarterly meetings instead of monthly. This was a retreat. We really needed an involved board, so I kicked all the insiders off the board. A lot of them were big shareholders, and it really pissed them off. I took a stand and said, "We're gonna have an independent board, and we're gonna have mostly outside directors."

About the time I became CEO, I got a letter from a guy named Charlie Munger. He turned out to be Warren Buffett's vice chairman. His company had bought 10 or 11 percent of Lee, and I was worried that he was going to try to take over the company. I flew out to California with our investment banker to meet Charlie for the first time. I liked him, and it turned out that he was buying our stock for investment purposes only. It was the start of a good relationship. As luck would have it, we couldn't have had a better investor, counselor, and friend than Charlie and, tangentially, Warren Buffett. Through Charlie, I was able to bring a number of great independent directors to our company.

All in all, when I was approached to take the CEO's job, I knew I would face these challenges, but I also knew that I was as much interested in growing the company and taking care of all of our other stakeholders as I was in doing well by the shareholders. In my mind it isn't just all about the shareholders. You have a lot of people with a stake in an organization: consumers, employees, the community, your vendors, and more. I was determined to look at the company in its totality and to make the right decisions for all of them. And as I said, I wasn't scared. I was ready.

# CHAPTER 7

# Sea Change: Repositioning, Refocusing, and Renewing a Business

Many of the defining moments presented in this book are related to change—changes to corporate culture, personal career changes, changes to a company's business model.

Changing a company's culture or its business model takes a lot of courage and conviction. In most cases, however, the fundamental mission of the business remains intact. It is the execution of the mission that becomes problematic—an aspect of the business system has gone out of alignment.

The changes you will read about in this chapter are on a vastly different dimension. They are not about finding a better way to complete the company's mission—they are about finding a better mission. Some of these businesses utterly reinvented themselves. They didn't just attempt to turn the ship around—they took the ship apart and turned it into an airplane. It's one thing to change the way you go about competing in your market, and it's quite another to shift to a different market altogether.

I can personally relate to many of the change-driven stories in this book because in one way or another, throughout my business career, I either chose or was forced to take similar actions. I've cut costs, made career changes, changed the corporate culture, experimented with new concepts, and changed business models. But reinventing a company the way many of the executives in this chapter did is beyond the scope of anything I experienced. Indeed, the following stories are on the outer edge of the spectrum of a business's response to change.

After reading the stories in this chapter, it's easy to conclude that these leaders charted the right course. But imagine the corporate environment as it existed when these decisions were being made, and it's not hard to summon up a loud chorus of doubters in virtually every case. It probably appeared as if these executives were grasping at straws as they searched for a new mission—a new foundational principle.

Perhaps one of the most difficult things to do in business is move ahead with a difficult decision despite the critics. Sometimes they are a lot louder than the supporters. I know there are leaders out there who never show any doubt. It's always full steam ahead with them. But I've never met a thoughtful CEO who didn't wonder quietly once in a while if he was moving the company in the right direction. It can be difficult to figure out what to do with the doubters. Not the people themselves, but their arguments, concerns, and logic. If you don't own up to your company's weaknesses and threats, you can't address them—and they are not going to magically self-correct. As any trial attorney will tell you: be as familiar with the opposing counsel's argument as you are with your own. When you really understand the contrary position, only then can you figure out how to neutralize it.

There are a lot of ways to perform business psychoanalysis. As suggested in the previous chapter, you take a hard look at who you are and where you are, and then measure that against where you want to be. One tool that can be very useful is SWOT analysis, which looks at a company's Strengths, Weaknesses, Opportunities, and Threats. It's a tool that can be used to help chart a company's direction. Using a specific strategic goal as a starting point, the analysis studies various business dimensions. The company's strengths and weaknesses are an internal analysis: What does the company do well in relation to the achievement of the goal? What are the company's weaknesses? Then the analysis goes outside the company: What are the opportunities? What are the threats?

Then you ask yourself how it all matches up. For example, does your company have the strengths to take advantage of the opportunities and neutralize the threats? If not, can the company shore up those areas? SWOT analysis is a valuable tool only if done honestly, without exaggeration one way or another. And it's an "as is" analysis, not a way of compiling a wish list. If you can't fight the threats, or if the opportunities are not as big as they need to be, then it is time, as this analysis shows you, for some tough decisions.

Whether or not the executives in this chapter used SWOT analysis or some variation on it or simply had an internal calculus, they all came to a moment of truth after weighing the factors and concluded that a new direction was in order. Sometimes the new direction was a matter of refocusing the existing business; sometimes it involved shedding businesses that didn't fit into the strategic equation; and sometimes the only viable direction seemed to be moving into an entirely new market. Ron Shaich sold Au Bon Pain not because the restaurant chain was a poor performer, but because it was internally competing for attention and resources with another emerging business line he felt had greater growth potential, Panera Bread Company. Shaich had a strong vision for Panera and knew it wasn't going to get there if he continued to serve two masters.

A lot of people have a vision for the future, but few have the ability, fortitude, and position to redirect an entire business toward that vision. Each of the executives in this chapter placed a big bet on a new direction. But all of these corporate turnarounds, whether through repositioning, refocusing, or renewing, were triggered by a tough, isolating business decision that these leaders now describe, in retrospect, as their defining moment.

## RICHARD MAHONEY
**Chairman and CEO, Monsanto Company**

The chemical industry was experiencing a decline, and Monsanto was no different. The company, as Richard Mahoney found it, had difficulty making a profit, and Wall Street had noticed.

Wanting to build a great company, Mahoney set out to change all that. In what became his defining moment, he began to make a series of dramatic business moves to turn the corporate ship around and set it on a new course. He sold off billions of dollars of low-growth, low-profit companies in the firm's portfolio, and he devised a long-term plan to move into high-growth, high-margin businesses. His goal: to transform Monsanto from a chemicals company into a life sciences, agriculture, and pharmaceuticals company.

Refocusing the company was not an easy task. Mahoney poured billions of dollars into his new businesses knowing that it would be years before he saw a return on that money. In the meantime, he had to keep Wall Street under control, as it was not happy with the company's performance during Mahoney's refocusing efforts.

Mahoney stuck to his guns, and in time his vision for a new Monsanto came to fruition in what turned out to be one of the most dramatic transformations in American corporate history.

IF THERE'S ONE thing I've learned in business, it is that you have to continually remake yourself.

When I went to Monsanto in 1962, the company was in the petrochemical business, where we used petroleum as a base to create new products: plastics, resins, and products used in agriculture such as herbicides.

If you look at the history of the chemical industry, much of it really got going in the 1930s when cars and oil and gas were really starting to grow. Petrochemicals were left over from refining gasoline. They were cheap and were very reactive. Companies like Monsanto, DuPont, and Dow would buy ten cents' worth of petrochemicals, add forty cents' worth of value to them, and make a ton of money selling plastics, fibers, and "polyvinyl everythings." The business in the '40s and '50s was based on this low-cost, very reactive material. In fact, at that time the chemical industry was one of the hot stock sectors.

Then something changed in the '60s and '70s. The oil companies started to see the value in their feedstock, started doing more with it, created a market, and were able to get a better price for it. And the oil countries got interested in upgrading and building up their infrastructure. So what was ten cents of raw materials with forty cents of value added became forty cents of raw materials with ten cents of value added.

The whole world was changing. Monsanto was still plugging away. The company had just formed a major joint venture with Conoco to provide them with feedstock for plastics and other products. But it was obvious that this game was over and that the power was going into the hands of the oil companies and the oil-producing countries.

The core of Monsanto was in serious jeopardy, and it was subject to the swings in oil prices. There are two sides to that. In the '73 or

'74 period, when the price of oil went through the roof, the products based on [oil] went very well. Monsanto, for one year, made a 20 percent return on equity for the first time in recent memory. But I wanted us to be in charge of our own future. I didn't want to have somebody else deciding whether we were going to make money that year.

There's a rule in the commodity chemical businesses—I've lectured on it—it's called the rule of twelve. There are twelve years of agony and then twelve months of enormous prosperity when the cycles all come together. It's just a cycle. Every CEO in these commodities businesses sees the same opportunity, expands like crazy, and then come twelve more years of agony.

When I became CEO in 1983, Monsanto was a chemical company with an agricultural group that was based on chemicals. I, like every new CEO, went to the mountain and said, "What is this all about? Who is it, Lord?" And the voice from up on top of the mountain, sounding like Milton Friedman, said, "It's the share owners, stupid!" So, I said, if I'm going to spend my life doing this, why not make a really great company? We started a great company strategy—we would be this great company in terms of financial performance and performance in society.

We set out to remake the company, and this became my defining moment and the defining moment for Monsanto as well. We decided to pull out of the chemical business—which had been moving away from us. We sold oil and gas investments. We sold tons of plastics businesses. We were the largest silicon wafer manufacturer in the country and we got rid of that. We systematically peeled them off. Over the course of the next several years, we sold something like $8 billion worth of businesses and bought another $3 billion or $4 billion.

We wanted to move into the life sciences area, which we were already in somewhat with our agriculture division and with initiatives started by my predecessor as CEO, Jack Hanley. The hope was that the field of agriculture would expand into biotechnology.

You have to figure out how to get into a business or gravitate toward it. You can't just fly your way in, it doesn't work. Those kinds of acquisitions invariably fail. You have to work your way to it, almost like an amoeba. You kind of surround it. Then you have to figure out what the drivers are—what makes the business go—and that takes a lot of good, talented people to figure that out. That's where strategic planning comes in.

We set out to buy a pharmaceutical company, but there weren't any for sale that were any good, and the ones that were good we couldn't afford. We had this big treasure chest of money from selling all those businesses. G. D. Searle and Company was rumored to be for sale. To get ready for it, we set up a pharmaceutical division and pulled together some disparate little businesses we had. We felt comfortable that we could move into pharma because of a strong background in agriculture: we had highly regulated products, long lead times, big R&D, a detail sales force—all these things were like pharmaceuticals. Then we bought a little company in Europe—for $60 million or $70 million I think we paid—because they could develop a couple of drugs for us, and we had some possible drugs of our own that we were fooling around with in the lab. Then we got comfortable with the field, hired a few people from the industry, and then we went after Searle. After a long, protracted negotiation with Don Rumsfeld, who was then running Searle, we bought them.

With the newly redefined company, we developed many new products, including genetically modified crops—it was the first time anybody had ever put a new property into a plant. So the agriculture group was moving into seeds, and we were also moving into pharmaceuticals. We got NutraSweet with Searle, which turned out to be a fabulous success and opened up some opportunities for us in the food business.

We decided to set up a freestanding series of companies. It was a very unusual organizational concept. We had a board of directors for Searle. I separated out NutraSweet into a company with its own board—outsiders and insiders. We also set up boards—all insiders—for the agriculture company and the remaining specialty chemical company. I was on all of the boards, so I could meddle without having to run them.

There were a few remaining chemical businesses, which we kept because they were very profitable: highly specialized plastics and a few other things—good margin businesses. They were a tremendous cash generator. They used to generate several hundred millions of cash, and we'd put some back into the plastics businesses and put the rest into biology.

During this time we invested in agriculture biotechnology for twelve years, knowing there'd be no new products until the mid-1990s. And my job was to keep Wall Street at bay. The pharmaceutical company Searle had the unique characteristic of being the only money-losing pharmaceutical company, and this was while we spent heavily on R&D for new products. We had to get all the earnings we could out of what we had in order to keep Wall Street happy. We poured tons of money into those businesses, and we knew there would be nothing coming for years. Wall Street thought this was terrible: "Profligate Spender," they used to call me. "You're spending all that money. Why don't you dispose of assets, turn off the lights, and go home?" But we kept plugging away, putting a lot of money into R&D at Searle, into R&D at the ag company.

By 1995 things had really developed. All the ag products we were working on hit. We reached 20 percent return on equity—as I had been promising. We had this whole raft of new ag products. We had our first pharmaceutical product, and Searle was now profitable.

So I retired—early. The board kept saying, "Why don't you

hang around a little bit and enjoy all this stuff?" And I said, I don't really want it, I'm sorry, I'd like to try something new. And I got out. I wound up over at the Weidenbaum Center at Washington University in St. Louis. I heard this somewhere: it's said that the first third of your life you learn, the second third you earn, and the third you return. So that's what I'm doing now. I'm here lecturing, counseling, and writing on business and public policy.

# LES LOEWE
## Chairman and CEO, Angelica Corporation

The Angelica Corporation that Les Loewe began working for in 1947 was in the work-apparel business. Its focus was manufacturing, marketing, and selling uniforms for workers in a variety of industries, including restaurants, hotels, and hospitals. The company also sold uniforms to railroad employees and workers in the food-processing industry.

From 1960 to 1980, Angelica acquired a number of small companies in the United States and Canada that amounted to a hodgepodge of uniform and linen businesses—a textile mill, small uniform-manufacturing firms, retail uniform stores, and mail-order marketers—all operating with varying degrees of effectiveness and profit. Supervising these businesses, a number of which should never have been acquired, was Loewe's job. He performed this role at a high level for nearly seven years, and he rose steadily at Angelica and was named CEO in 1980.

Les Loewe's defining moment took approximately one year to materialize, and it started after he determined that the Angelica uniform company needed to be repositioned and rebranded so that it could reach its potential. In the ensuing ten years, he more than succeeded as Angelica began to operate as a unified company with a strong corporate identity and a clear mission. Loewe managed to increase the company's annual sales to just short of $500 million and raise the share price from $3 to nearly $30.

———

WHEN I JOINED Angelica Uniform Company in 1947, our revenues were approximately $3 million per year. When we went public in 1958, they were about $9 million. Our business at Angelica was manufacturing and selling uniforms for restaurant workers, hotels, hospitals, and a variety of other markets.

After I was with the company for approximately fifteen years, we started acquiring other companies, most of them very small. We established a retail chain of uniform stores and had about three hundred stores at its peak. I became responsible for the management of those companies. We had about ten or twelve different operations. We had a mail-order operation. We also had a business of disposable textiles that are used in doctors' offices— paper patient gowns, and so on. We made special textile products for astronauts. We bought additional laundries, which provided linens to hospitals.

The uniform-manufacturing business was the most complicated of our businesses. Whenever we hired managers who came from the garment industry, they were lost in our kind of business. Most women's dress businesses require new product lines and new style lines every year, some two, three, or four times a year. With us, it was just the reverse: our customers wanted to be able to buy the same thing year after year after year. So the whole methodology of our business was entirely different.

When Angelica went public in 1958, we started out as an over-the-counter stock, then went to the American Stock Exchange. Then, as we grew, we were listed on the New York Stock Exchange.

The breakthrough event for the company as well as me
personally came when I decided we needed to position ourselves as
a health services company and to shed the market perception of us
simply as an apparel firm. We were performing well as a company,
but we quite clearly were neither leveraging our strengths nor
unlocking our potential value. Wall Street was blasé on the apparel
sector as a whole, and apparel firms were given low price-earnings
multiples. Although our business was heavily weighted to the health
services industry, we were primarily viewed as an apparel company.
What we needed to do was focus our brand and future growth on
the fast-growing and highly valued health services sector.

It took about a year from that initial realization to the market's
positive response. When I look back and take all of these events into
account, that decision, and the subsequent implementation of it, was
a defining achievement. We dramatically enhanced the value of our
stock and our perception in the marketplace.

And it was all true: more than half of our sales and revenues were
from health care. Our retail sales would be classified as sales to the
health care area. Our manufacturing business was a large seller to
hospitals, and our laundries were rented to hospitals. We had a lot
of health care volume, and we began to emphasize that in all of our
dealings with Wall Street, in our marketing, in our branding, and in
our growth plans.

After making the decision to reposition ourselves, it became
a major point of our focus. For example, we opened and operated
more laundries that serviced hospitals. Many hospitals had their
own laundries, and one of our main thrusts was to convince them
of the benefits of our service as opposed to operating laundries
in-house.

By concentrating our efforts in this area, we were able to
dramatically move our stock upwards. When I took over the
company, the stock was a little over $3 a share. When I left, it was

$29 to $30 a share. That was in ten years. And a big part of that was due to this particular realization, when I understood strategically what to focus on and how to leverage that in the marketplace.

# RONALD M. SHAICH
## Chairman and CEO, Panera Bread Company

Ron Shaich is an entrepreneur and professional businessman who has never stopped being a student. He learns and analyzes and thinks deeply before making a decision or embarking on a course of action. He is extremely passionate about his businesses, and he lives and dies with the ups and downs of his work.

As a college student, he devoted himself to creating a nonprofit community store after being falsely accused of shoplifting at a local convenience shop that students frequented. The store was wildly successful and became a model for other stores around the country—just an example of his creative business passion.

I have never met anyone quite like Ron Shaich in all my years in business. He likens his work as a businessman to art, especially the three-dimensional art of the sculptor, and he has certainly convinced me that there is a great deal of truth in this.

One of his "masterpieces" that most people will be familiar with is Au Bon Pain, the croissant and sandwich shop that can be found in major cities around the country.

While running Au Bon Pain, along with several other successful businesses, Shaich began to think that there was something wrong—or rather, that there was something very right and very wonderful hidden in his creation that needed to be brought into the light. His defining moment arrived when he took hammer and chisel to his companies, determined to reshape them and release into the world a new sculpture—a new business that had been hidden within the contours of the old one.

Today Panera Bread operates or franchises over 1,350 bakery-cafés in forty states and Canada.

————

CREATING A BUSINESS is like sculpture. You start with this block of nothing and you carve it. You're building, creating something. But if you look at it from one side—and this is actually what I find fascinating about business—you see one thing. Now you walk around ninety degrees, you see another view of it. Take, for example, Michelangelo's *David* in Florence. What a sculptor does is he's chiseling this block as he moves around, and he's continually working from all directions. In many ways, that's what a business is. It's three-dimensional, and, like a sculpture, people can relate to it whether they are insiders or outsiders.

The sculpture metaphor comes into play with my defining moment.

In 1993 Au Bon Pain had 250 stores. At that point I had begun to understand that the very things that made us successful also limited us. The reality of Au Bon Pain was that it was a wonderful niche business. We were great at being the best in a place between fine dining and fast food in high-density urban markets like Washington, New York, and Boston. We wouldn't have played in St. Louis.

Buried in everything good is something bad; buried in everything bad is something good. This is something I actually deeply believe. It's the reality of life and business. Over ten years, we had been able to grow the business—grow our profits—25 percent each year. The problem was that we couldn't continue like that. It would have meant another fifty stores a year—and remember, this was a niche business.

I'm friends with a lot of people, and back in 1993 I was asked to meet a couple of guys from St. Louis who at that time owned a nineteen-store chain doing a million dollars a unit called the St. Louis Bread Company. I met with them; I spent hours trying to help them understand where they were and how they could grow their business. We became friends, and one thing led to another. I was intrigued by their business. It seemed to me like a fourth business we could run along with Au Bon Pain, our international business, and our dough-manufacturing business.

In many ways St. Louis Bread Company was a conduit to the suburban marketplace. And in November of 1993, we bought it, and we paid $23 million for it.

We left the business alone for two years and studied it. There was a tremendous amount of learning that occurred in those years that became the genesis of everything we're doing here at Panera.

But by 1995, we started to play with the Bread Company, and we applied all of our learning. An encapsulation of that learning is that the world is changing. In a world in which everything becomes commoditized, where everything is processed, there are extraordinary opportunities for people who can create things that other people perceive as special. You saw it in beer, you saw it in coffee—you didn't have to be very smart to see it—you saw it in soft drinks. We understood that the same thing was going to happen in food service, and in fact the same thing was happening in bread. So we put the two together.

Bread was the thing that defined our authority. It wasn't that we were just trying to sell bread; bread gave customers a cue that told them what kind of people we are. If you wear a tie, you're not wearing it because you like wearing a silly piece of colored silk around your neck. You're wearing it because you're trying to give me a cue about yourself, that you're a professional and many other things. The tie speaks to your authority. That's what bread does, because if we can make and serve great bread, that tells customers a lot about who we are and where we're coming from.

So we start playing it out. In 1996 we add a bagel line; we move into the breakfast business. Individual store volumes popped from $1 million to $1.25 million; the profits were way up. In 1997 we changed everything about the company. First we changed the core product, the bread. We changed the environment. We had this vision for it that we're trying to deliver against: it's our "concept essence," which we call "Gathering Place." It's creating environments where people want to sit. The price of admission becomes our food, so that was our second change. Third, we changed the name of the concept because we discovered as we were expanding out of St. Louis that the name St. Louis Bread Company has limits. "St. Louis" really represents Clydesdales and beer to many people. We changed it to Panera Bread, which is an empty vessel we can put our new identity into. And then also we start franchising. Volume pops from $1.25 million to $1.75 million.

It was very clear to me that this is really a powerful thing. But I was in a lot of pain because it was just one of four divisions in the company. I had professional managers running the divisions, and I realized that Panera would never get the resources and attention and care it needed. It was a gem being hidden in this company, and it needed every ounce of our financial and human resources. I couldn't solve the problem.

Now we're getting closer to the defining moment. I had presidents at every one of these divisions. Everybody was fighting, whining at each other. The guys in Au Bon Pain were upset—they were saying, "Why are you taking cash from us and putting it out there?" The guys out here—at Panera—they didn't have a clue what was going to hit them, no sense of the infrastructure that was going to be needed. The guys in manufacturing, they were off on their own agenda. The guys in international never called home.

I realized that this was a gem, and I felt that its potential was going to get wasted. I didn't know what to do with it.

I was away over the holidays, and I was talking about this and about how upset I was. And somebody said to me, "Ron, what would you do with the business if the name of the company wasn't Au Bon Pain but was Panera Bread? And what would you do with all those other divisions?"

I thought for one second.

And I said, "You know what? Panera is the gem. Taking care of it is everything. I would sell everything else, monetize everything else, take everything—take the very best people, all of our resources, and bet it all on Panera. In fact, if we don't do that, the greatest risk is we're going to destroy it. This is the gem."

What happened next was my defining moment.

Au Bon Pain was in many ways my first work of art; it was my first child. Call it whatever metaphor you want, it was an extension of me. These were people I had grown up with who I cared about; this was a business that I worked on for fifteen years. It was not something you just simply say, "Okay, I'm going to move dollars from here to there—move dollars to Panera." It was the hardest decision of my life. At this point we are a public company; the stock's been flat for three years; the Internet is starting to boom; everybody's telling me I'm washed up. It was really a tough, personal struggle. And the question was, "How do I make sense of all this?"

And so, my defining moment wasn't the thought process—it was being able to stay with it through all the conflict and pain and noise as everything played out. The long and the short of it was that I made the decision to focus on Panera, and it then took us a year and a half to sell every other business. That was horrendous, just because it was being played out in front of all these people—employees, friends, investors.

The end of the story is that we did it and we did it well. The stock's been up fifteenfold since. Panera Bread has been the top-performing company in the restaurant industry for the last decade.

The punch line is that everything depends on how you look at it. Going back to my sculpture metaphor, if you look at a sculpture just from the front, you might completely misread it. Because you're just looking at one dimension, right? You have to continue to walk around it. And that's what I did with the business. The powerful thing for me was in understanding—in thinking of Panera not as a division of the company, but thinking of it as an entity that needed to be nurtured in its own right. Thinking about it differently, but with the *same exact* set of facts, thinking about them differently—that created an answer to the problem. That was the defining *intellectual* moment, however. The defining *emotional* moment was going through everything I just described—the playing out of the situation.

You may know when something's right—the right thing to do—but many of us, as human beings, put off doing something about it because of the emotional strings that are attached. Addressing it head-on, though, is the only way to take control and make something of it.

# FREDERIC V. SALERNO
### Vice Chairman and CFO, Verizon; President and CEO, New York Telephone Company

Frederic Salerno's father, an electrician, gave his son some important advice. He told Frederic that he didn't want him working with his hands, as he had done throughout his life, but rather with his head.

Salerno took the advice seriously, winning a college scholarship

through the Electricians' Union, as did his two brothers, and he
went on to earn a degree as an electrical engineer.

When he first joined New York Telephone Company in 1965
in an entry-level position, he did work with his hands for a time
while he learned the business. But then his head took over and he
rose to the top. His defining moment occurred when he and Ivan
Seidenberg saw the future of telecommunications and made the
decision to begin a radical makeover of the phone company.

By the time Salerno and Seidenberg were finished, they had
transformed the telephone industry from a stodgy old landline
business into a dynamic, modern communications giant for the
digital age that encompassed wireless voice and data services,
Internet, broadband, digital delivery of television, movie, and music
programming, and more.

A masterful conceptualizer and strategist, Salerno lived his
father's advice and as a result brought his company into a new era—
and brought his customers there as well.

---

I HAVE LOVED every job I had from the day I joined the old New
York Telephone Company in 1965 as a young person twisting and
splicing wires, learning about the business, to the day I became
president and CEO of the company in 1987, and all of the jobs
that came after, including vice chairman of Verizon. I was blessed
to wake up every morning loving to go to work. Every job was
challenging and unique, and I had great bosses and mentors.

The most important and impactful decision I was ever a
part of occurred when we realized NYNEX needed a profound
strategic shift. We were the first company from the old Bell system
companies to realize we had to change. Our company, NYNEX,
was formed out of the old Baby Bells in 1984 by joining New
York Telephone together with New England Telephone. We were

stuck in the low-growth northeastern region of the country. The macroeconomics were not very good at all. We were a very highly regulated business. We knew we had to change.

Ivan Seidenberg was the chairman of NYNEX, and he was a great boss—we've functioned as teammates since 1991. At one time we were in a contest to win the chairman's job, and Ivan got it. But we continued to work together hand in glove, and we changed the course of the phone business.

Over the years we did six big mergers that define the business today. The first merger was in 1997 with Bell Atlantic. We were the first regional company to merge.

We merged because, back then, Ivan and I saw the need of expanding our business by combining with another company that was very, very strong. We gave a presentation to our board of directors at NYNEX. Just the two of us worked on this. I gave the presentation. Basically we said we had to take a couple of steps.

Number one, we had to grow more horizontally. One way was to merge with Bell Atlantic. Bell Atlantic's region was mostly the mid-Atlantic states, New Jersey all the way down to Virginia. We also shared the lucrative New York market with them. We hadn't even talked to Bell Atlantic. Yet we knew it would be one of the most important national mergers.

Number two, we had to grow our cellular unit. This meant we had to do a merger with a wireless company. We didn't know exactly which one that was, but we said most likely it would be the Air Touch Corporation.

Number three, we had to move up the food chain—get larger in general and get into more products and services, data products, enterprise products. This would be vertical growth, not just horizontal.

Nobody had done any of this at that time. The regional Bells had not merged. There were no cellular mergers at the time. Basically we said, "Here's where we are now. It ain't gonna cut it in our slow-growth, highly regulated areas. We need to break out of this geographical footprint; we need to make it larger, and we need to provide more products and services, such as cellular."

I'll never forget, after that presentation, we had a couple of new directors who had just come in, and they said, "Oh, my God! Is this what you guys do at every board meeting? I thought I joined the board of a stodgy, regulated business, but obviously that's not the case."

We got the decision to move ahead with the plan, and the first step was that we merged our cellular business with Bell Atlantic— not the entire business, just our cellular business—to see how well we got along with them. It was a great success. It was a very good cellular operation, and Bell Atlantic had terrific managers. It went well, and after that we announced the merger of the entire company—Bell Atlantic with NYNEX.

It got a lot of press and a lot of scrutiny. A lot of people were saying that there was a violation of antitrust law, but of course that wasn't the case. Basically they ran their business and we ran our business—we weren't overlapping. Finally the Department of Justice agreed, and we formed our company. It truly was a merger of equals, although they got the name Bell Atlantic, which Ivan and I liked better than NYNEX. They agreed to move all their headquarters operations up to the New York area. So we never had to move. Basically we were on the same floor, same building, and the people from Bell Atlantic came up. The chairman of Bell Atlantic became the chairman of NYNEX for a year, but then our chairman, Ivan Seidenberg, took over.

As time went on we looked at the strategy, the blueprint, and said, All right, time for the next step: to grow the business in various new products and services. GTE came along, and they had great enterprise business products and services to sell that helped businesses operate better. They also had a big cellular business. We merged with them. It was one of the largest mergers in history. We changed our name from Bell Atlantic to Verizon. We didn't take the GTE name; we didn't take the Bell Atlantic name. We got a firm to help us come out with a new name, Verizon, which really happened to be very well accepted by the marketplace. In terms of our jobs, the same thing happened as before: I stayed the vice chair and CFO of planning, and Ivan gave up the chairman spot for one year to Chuck Lee of GTE. When Chuck Lee retired, Ivan took over the entire operation.

Then the last merger in this series was with Vodaphone— their U.S. wireless operations. If you go back to 1997, we said we were going to do it with Vodaphone—right on that chart it said we were going to do it with our cellular operation. And sure enough, it ended up we did it. Actually, it had a different name back then, but it was the same assets we were talking about. And that turned out, I think, to be the most impactful merger that Verizon has ever made, because right now about half of Verizon's business is that wireless business we created. The other half, of course, is the wire line business.

I worked with Ivan on all these deals, but generally I was the lead negotiator. What we always tried to do was set aside emotions and try to understand what the other side was trying to accomplish and respect that. Doing it that way, we were able to get what we needed accomplished.

We knew that the world was changing. We knew in 1997 that we weren't going to be the same company that we were then. We knew it was going to require a lot of flexibility in every way. We knew it might mean personal sacrifices. There was no guarantee what my position would be after all the mergers. But that didn't stop me.

When you merge, you make combinations, and some things fall out. But at the end of all of this, we ended up where Ivan was the chair and I was one of the vice chairs.

In the end, we built a world-class business. We created what is still the best wireless company out there.

# HANS STERNBERG
## Chairman, Starmount Life Insurance Company

Retailing is in Hans Sternberg's DNA. For as long as he can remember, his family have been merchants, first selling their goods from a general store they operated in Germany.

The family left Germany and their business, however, before the start of World War II, fleeing from the Nazis and immigrating to the United States.

Once in the States, the family quickly returned to its roots, buying a department store called Goudchaux's in Baton Rouge, Louisiana. Sternberg's mother, father, and siblings all worked in the store in order to make it a success. And they were successful. Growing and expanding through acquisitions, they created the largest family-owned department store chain in the country.

With the growth of the stores came the opportunity to offer and experiment with other kinds of products and services, one of them being insurance. Sternberg's defining moment occurred when an insurance company whose policies he was planning to sell reneged on a promise. The moment initiated a remarkable transformation of the family business, eventually moving it completely out of retailing and into the insurance industry.

Sternberg's story and his defining moment exemplify the American Dream, as does the family work ethic that began on another continent many generations ago and is still apparent today. Along with his wife and children, Sternberg continues the family tradition of working hard together in a mutual, rewarding, and successful endeavor.

———

MY FAMILY OWNED a general store in a small town in Germany near the Dutch border. The store had been there since the 1700s. My family operated that store, and when Hitler began his policies of discrimination, we left Germany in 1936 for the United States. I was one year old when we left. After looking around for a business to buy here in the U.S., my father visited a cousin in New Orleans who was in the apparel-manufacturing business. My father told him that what he really wanted to do was buy and operate a store. In 1937 my cousins were able to find him one to purchase in Baton Rouge, Louisiana, called Goudchaux's.

After college and the navy, I joined my father and brother in the store, and we developed it into a fairly large company. We bought Maison Blanche Department Stores and in 1987 changed the name of the company itself to Maison Blanche.

We became the largest family-owned department store chain in the country, with 24 department stores, having an average size of 150,000 square feet. We operated in Louisiana and Florida. At one time we had about 8,800 employees. We had 640,000 charge accounts. As we grew, we developed a financial wing. We also had travel agencies.

We started selling insurance to our charge account customers. At first we were just an agency, and we had someone take the courses to qualify to be an agent. We worked with insurance companies and sold their products to our charge account customers, which numbered about 100,000 at the time. Over time, we developed as an insurance agency that would sell to customers and suppliers and anyone else interested in insurance, not just charge account customers. We sold property, casualty, and life insurance.

There was a need among our customers for a modest amount of life insurance at low cost. The insurance company that had the best policy was located in Donaldsonville, Louisiana, and was named Security Life. I called and told them my agents wanted to sell their life insurance product, and the head of the insurance company agreed. I announced it to my sales force—there were maybe ten people involved, and they were all trained on the product. We announced it with a bit of fanfare.

Then, three days before we were supposed to begin selling, the gentleman from Security Life called and said he couldn't let us sell the product. He said he had two hundred agents, and they were very nervous that we were too big. They thought Goudchaux's was too big to compete against, and they were afraid we would take all of their customers.

I got a little angry about that. I was embarrassed because I had been told we would be selling the policy and had announced it to my staff. Now, all of a sudden, we couldn't do what I said we were going to do.

At that time I made a pledge to myself that this type of thing wouldn't happen to me again. Because I was so angry, I decided I would just start my own life insurance company. Then I wouldn't be dependent upon someone else for what I could or could not do. I felt somewhat betrayed or abused. And when I felt taken advantage of, I took action.

It turned out to be a threshold event in my business career.

We started the insurance company with $400,000 in capital, which was the amount required by the Louisiana Department of Insurance. The company has always been nicely profitable. Next year we will do $54 million in premiums.

I have since sold the department stores. It was a business decision that I made, and it was the correct one.

Turning a negative into a positive is always a lot of fun. Sometimes getting angry at something and doing something about it—if your anger is properly channeled and properly derived— allows you to turn the situation into something better. It can be character-building.

I tell people not to be afraid to get angry. You know, sometimes the question is, What do I do with that anger? Do I use it to press ahead or do I just sulk?

Just letting your emotions go is not the way. You've got to think your way through it.

## SUSAN S. ELLIOTT

**Founder, Chairman, and CEO, Systems Service Enterprises, Inc. (SSE)**

E ducation has always played a big role in Susan Elliott's life—that is, both educating others and being educated herself. She still recalls the time when she was enrolled in a grade school where two grades, the fourth and the fifth, were held in the same classroom. She began in the fourth grade, but her teacher suggested that she really belonged in the fifth, so she just moved her desk across the room, "and there I was," she recalls, "suddenly a fifth-grader." It was a special moment.

She loved learning about math and numbers, but chose an American Studies major at Smith College, hoping not to pigeonhole herself and narrow her education. But what she really wanted to do, this being the 1950s, was to find a job that didn't require her to go to typing school. She found it at IBM, which was just starting to look for women with analytical and logical abilities to train on its new computing systems. She took a test that IBM offered and eventually landed a job. The learning began anew as she became a programmer and eventually a systems analyst with account responsibility.

Elliott's career path eventually led her to start her own consulting business, offering her computer and programming savvy to clients, initially as an IBM partner. Because the business concept, the computers, and the software were all so new, Elliott was often only one or two steps ahead of her clients in learning the programs. But her defining moment arrived when she decided to turn her energies and her company in a new direction: education.

Elliott's defining moment propelled her into the new world of computer education, and her company, SSE, became a pioneer in the fledgling industry of teaching and training individuals to perform tasks on personal computers.

They had to figure out what the format, schedule, and curriculum should be and how to teach in the classrooms. Motivated by the excitement of new learning and driven by the desire to educate her clients and solve their problems, Elliott turned her small training company into a highly successful computer and high-tech learning company.

SSE has evolved today to offer additional services in software application development and network infrastructure. In addition, Susan Elliott is a former chair of the Federal Reserve Bank of St. Louis.

———

MY FIRST JOB out of college, in the summer of 1958, was with IBM, and I had eleven weeks of training, from 8:00 AM until 5:00 PM. It was like a full college course. They gave us only one week on computers—in the tenth week—and told us that the average person wouldn't need any more training than that because there were not going to be that many computers. That was IBM in 1958!

So I took it upon myself as best I could to learn how to program a computer, and gradually I grew into the position of a systems analyst with account responsibility. IBM had big computers at the major St. Louis corporations, and one of my key clients was Monsanto, where I helped design systems. Other big clients were Anheuser-Busch and International Shoe Company.

I became pregnant in 1966, and IBM wanted me to stay at home for three months because I was so "fragile." I just couldn't do that, so instead I started my own business. At that time, you really couldn't put a woman's name on a company, so I went with SSE, which stood for Systems Service Enterprises. At IBM they used to call us "systems service" representatives, so I began with that and added "Enterprises," which would give me the liberty to do other things as the business grew. My thought was that if International Business Machines could be IBM, then surely Systems Service Enterprises could be SSE! SSE also happens to be my initials.

I freelanced from 1966 until 1983, in the later years working part-time for a bank implementing its systems. It was in 1983 that my company really began. My husband and I went to an Arts and Education Council auction, and one of the auction items was an IBM PC. IBM came out with the original PC at the end of 1981, so it had been on the market for a little more than a year. I said to Howard, "Can you imagine having a computer in our home?" It was an astounding thought at the time. Bless his heart, he raised his hand, and we bid against our friend Don Danforth, and we got the PC. We were walking out that night, and Don said to me, "What are you going to do with that PC?" and I said to him, "I'm going to revive my business."

I was awake all night because I was so excited; I couldn't wait to get started. I gave notice at the bank. Three weeks' notice, as I recall. My last day there was June 24, 1983. The following Monday morning, June 27, I was in my basement with the computer on my makeshift desk—a big piece of plywood, a lightbulb in the center of the ceiling, and the washer and dryer running in the background. In terms of growing the business and my 100 percent commitment to the business, it all began on that day.

When I revived SSE in 1983, I thought of myself as just getting into the consulting business. That's what I knew how to do. That's what I had done at IBM. I became a partner of IBM's in November of that year. They had a new retail store, and we came in as consultants. Individuals and small businesses for the first time could spend something like $5,000 and get a machine with an IBM—Big Blue—logo on it. Customers would come into that store and say to the IBM salesman, "What do I buy? What do I need?"

The salesman would sell to them and then say, "SSE will come out and install it for you and show you how to use it." And that is what we did; no one ever asked for a reference.

We got started as consultants, as I didn't know any other approach and I didn't have a business plan. In fact, in thinking about it today, probably every big decision that I made was spontaneous as opposed to having this very mapped-out, serious business plan.

Two people were key to our relaunch and subsequent growth. One was an assistant superintendent in the Ladue School District, a local public school system. She came to me and said, "You know, we're getting these IBMs (as opposed to Apple computers), and nobody knows how to use them. I want the district to think that this is a good decision to purchase the ten IBMs. So what do you think? Would you like to teach on them at night? Train people on how to use them? That way we can bring in some revenue, and that would be important to the district."

I scratched my head and said, "Sure, I guess so . . . why not!"

But before committing, I talked to several other people. The second key person I talked to was the head of Mary Institute, a well-known private school in the area, who said, "I think getting into training is really important. People are going to have to be trained on how to use these things."

That did it for me. Right then I made the decision to get into training and education and changed the future course of my company.

Then we had to figure out how to write courseware—we had to figure out the format, schedule, and a curriculum. We determined the format should be four three-hour sessions, such as four Monday nights in a row. We knew it couldn't be a semester because business-people can't commit for that long. It had to be three hours because you couldn't teach any of the concepts well in just one hour. It had to be long enough to shape a concept or a message.

Then the big thing happened: the Ladue school district began advertising the training programs. It was named Hi-U, and they used the Charlie Chaplin figure that had been IBM's spokesperson in its ads. Ladue advertised all of our courses; we provided all of the sweat equity. Ladue had the money to do the advertising, and we did all the work. The partnership probably helped us become the leading training company in the St. Louis region.

We brought in some technical people (early "eager beavers") who could figure out how to do the training. We started with a basic course that covered: What is a PC? What is a floppy disk? What does the word "hardware" mean? What does the word "software" mean? It was that basic. We had to have four people registered to hold the class. Occasionally, I'd put my husband in the class because it was less expensive to enroll him than to cancel the class. I remember one time he came home and said, "You know, that guy seems to really know what he's talking about." We were dealing with a few companies—one such was Graybar—but mostly individuals who wanted to learn. Ladue and I wrote a joint letter to every CEO of every large corporation in St. Louis to drum up business. That's how we got started, and the learning evolved from there.

Companies were slow to recognize that they would need to train their employees, but eventually they came around. We had three PCs where we started our own daytime training in our first real office. Then we moved to our next location, where we had two classrooms with ten desks and ten PCs. It was imperative that each student have his/her own PC. Later we had five classrooms going.

The pattern I saw was that when new software came out, the demand for training would peak dramatically. Then, as the software matured and Microsoft delayed coming out with a new version of a program, companies would pull it in-house and train for themselves. Back then it was first about MicroPro's WordStar and then IBM's Displaywriter, Lotus, and WordPerfect. Most of the large corporations in St. Louis became our clients, such as Emerson, Monsanto, and Southwestern Bell. We stayed with only the most popular software. We never got into Apple because there wasn't enough of a market. They had something like 7 percent market share.

We also made a number of acquisitions. We bought the book of business of one training company and integrated another training company into ours, Productivity Plus. Later, as we were evolving, we bought Pure Logics, a consulting and software development company.

We are now over $10 million in revenues, with about 110 employees, and we develop courseware—eLearning—for our clients who want to deliver their training worldwide over the Internet. We just brought in a big Boeing contract, and we had to hire 28 people to meet their needs—that's awesome for us.

What's true with us is true in every industry, but especially in information technology: you have to be just ahead of the curve and start to innovate while you're still thinking that things are really great, rather than wait until later. You don't have the luxury of enjoying significant market share before you decide you have to change, again. My favorite expression through the years has been, "There is nothing as constant as change!"

To that point, SSE has evolved today to offering three core services: eLearning/blended learning, software application development, and network infrastructure.

# CHAPTER 8

# When to Fold 'Em: Knowing When It's Time to Step Aside

I knew it was time to go. It used to be that I couldn't wait for Monday to arrive so I could get back to the office and jump into the thick of things. I loved what I was doing. I enjoyed the people, and I thrived on the challenge of business in all its forms. I loved visiting the stores, reviewing the numbers, scouting locations, analyzing the competition, looking for new opportunities. It was a way of life. I did this for twenty-one years, and it never got old. Some people—maybe most people—would describe me as a workaholic. I would leave the house early in the morning, try to make it home by dinner, and after dinner I worked at my desk at home until late into the night, clicking away at my electronic adding machine and checking the daily numbers. I thrived on this. I didn't know any other way, and I didn't want to.

Over the course of my career, I had seen a lot. I appreciated my experiences even as I was going through them—I didn't have to wait for retrospection to kick in. During my tenure at Medicare-Glaser, the company expanded, was sold, was reacquired in a leveraged buyout, went public, and was sold again. It was all very exciting, fun, and rewarding.

Things started to change for me after the second sale of the company. This was a difficult transaction. The process took much longer than I anticipated, and up until the very end I didn't know if the sale was going to close. We finally worked it out, but it was an unnecessarily challenging and draining experience.

After the transaction, I took over running Express Scripts, the joint venture we had launched between Medicare-Glaser and New York Life Insurance Company. It was a great concept, and I knew it had tremendous potential. Even realizing this, I had to work too hard to enjoy the work. For the first time in my life, my passion for business had waned. The thrills and the sense of accomplishment no longer accompanied me on my way to work and on my way home. Instead of excitedly wanting Mondays to come, I looked forward to Fridays. This was not like me. I was officially burned out. It was time for me to leave.

Most people stay in business for as long as they can for financial reasons. But for those who have a choice, it can be a difficult task to recognize when it's time to step away. If you follow sports, you're familiar with the common story of the top athlete who sticks around for several seasons beyond his prime, while fans boisterously criticize him for not bowing out gracefully. In short, people who have dedicated their lives to something don't easily give up what could be the single greatest contributor to their sense of identity and sense of purpose. It's the same with businesspeople. They are competitive by nature. No one wants to admit that they can no longer operate at a high level, or that they've lost their business superpowers, or, perish the thought, that they're no longer needed. And certainly, no one wants to stick around so long that eventually they are shown the door, by either their boss or their board.

It takes tough introspection to recognize when it's time to move on. I had a senior executive, our director of store operations, whose time had passed. He couldn't fathom the new things we required of him—technologies, systems, analyses. He was a good person, a good businessman, and a loyal employee. I didn't have the heart to let him go and struggled with it for some time. Finally, I just had to do it. Once the decision was made, he admitted to me, partly relieved, that the business had passed him by and that the new ways of doing business were over his head.

With today's technology cycles, it doesn't take long for a successful and seasoned executive to feel completely out of touch with key operational technologies, customers, or vendors. Experience cannot be overrated, so I'm not trying to shove every technically challenged businessperson (like me) out the door, but knowledge of the modes of communication that your customers, vendors, partners, and society in general are using is an invaluable tool of the trade. I know some top executives who still don't feel comfortable using e-mail—and if it wasn't for my grandchildren showing me what to do, I might not either. As we all get older, we've got to keep up or risk becoming dinosaurs.

My experience with my own retirement and that of others has taught me some lessons. If a company doesn't have a mandatory retirement policy, it is important that it have a system in place for evaluating the competency of employees. If nothing else, it gives a reluctant boss like me the information needed to make decisions. Furthermore, a company must recognize that when someone hangs around too long and becomes a roadblock to the advancement of others, people who are hardworking, smart, and ambitious can be discouraged from staying with the company. Treasures can be lost.

In this chapter, we meet two executives who knew how to orchestrate their closing act in business. It took planning, confidence in their successors, an awareness of their limitations, and a sense of purpose for their lives after business. Each did it in his own style. The lessons in these stories, however, are not limited to the final grand exit; these are lessons for any transition. Planning the move, establishing the factors that trigger it, and understanding what will drive the next phase—these are as important for individual moves as for corporate ones. Because no matter the circumstances, when you make a change, it's better to do it on your own terms than on anyone else's.

## GEORGE HERBERT WALKER III
### Chairman and CEO, Stifel, Nicolaus & Company,
### U.S. Ambassador to Hungary

Bert Walker is a persistent man. He never gives up, despite setbacks, despite disappointments. Probably the most significant setback he ever experienced was when he was rebuffed by his father in his attempt to convince his dad that it was his time to run the family business, the investment banking firm of G. H. Walker & Company.

While very disappointed, Walker remained loyal to his father but was still determined to make a mark for himself. He settled into a subordinate role and worked hard to make a difference in the company.

Walker's time did come, but only when he left the confines of the family business after it had been merged into a larger company. Walker later joined a different firm, Stifel, Nicolaus & Company. After only two and a half years, he was rewarded for his contributions by being named president and chief executive officer and later chairman of the board. Now he had the opportunity to lead a business and he did so with gusto. He grew the company, made numerous smart acquisitions, and built Stifel's capital markets and brokerage business.

As successful as he was, Walker's defining moment is not about his accomplishments in business, but about leaving the business world behind and beginning his life's second act at age sixty-one. With fortunate timing, he chose the moment to end the business phase of his life, placed the business (with one setback you will read about) in the hands of a superb successor, and began a new life devoted to family, community, and national service.

––––––––

MY BUSINESS EXPERIENCE started in September 1958 when I joined our family firm, G. H. Walker & Company, as a registered representative. It was an investment banking firm started by my grandfather, the original George Herbert Walker, in St. Louis in 1900.

My most important decision came years later, in 1992, when I decided I would not continue as the chief executive officer of the investment banking firm I was then running and handed over the reins to a successor.

Of course, a lot went on between those two events.

While working at G. H. Walker & Company in 1963, I left St. Louis to start a Chicago office for the company. My work there went very well, so well in fact that a family adviser (my dad's minister) came to Chicago and suggested to me that it was time for me to talk to my dad about my moving east (headquarters by that time were in New York) and taking over the leadership of the firm.

My father was not friendly to this idea. He said, "Well, let me think about it." And six months later, he gave me his decision: "You know, I just don't think you're ready for that yet."

I believed that in his view I would never be ready, so I decided to move back from Chicago to St. Louis and settle down there, where our family roots were (parents and grandparents were native St. Louisans). In March of 1971, I moved back to St. Louis to assume the leadership role in our branch office. A year later, we changed from a partnership to a corporation, and I was urged by the younger partners to become chairman of the company—a role my father held and gave up unhappily.

I soon found out that being chairman in a branch office meant practically nothing except that I sat at the end of the table at our directors' meetings in New York while the firm was being managed by the executive group in the headquarters office.

Eventually, hard times came to our firm, and for many small firms, when the New York Stock Exchange put restrictions on us. Negotiable commissions were introduced, and fixed commissions were no longer enforceable. Our net worth diminished to less than $3 million. My father, still the largest shareholder, had to sell the firm or we'd go under. So we were acquired at the end of 1974 by White, Weld & Company, a major New York international investment firm.

My father told me, "Now listen, we're making this deal with White, Weld, and as a part of family loyalty and ethics, you've got to stay with White, Weld for at least a year, whether you want to or not. I really insist on that." So I said, "Okay."

I was made a senior vice president and a member of the board at White, Weld & Company, and I stayed a year to the day. But I was told by various people that I didn't have a bright future there. Some of my contemporaries who had moved over from G. H. Walker & Company looked upon me as a rival and did not have positive feelings about me. I was told the chances of my moving up were not very good (in fact, negligible), so I should really look around for another opportunity. Since at that time I was the sole support for five children and my financial resources were modest, it was not a happy period.

That's what I did. I ended up talking to a longtime family friend, George Newton, who was chairman and chief executive officer of Stifel, Nicolaus. He said, "Listen, if you want to come over to our firm, we'd love to have you. You can come in as executive vice president. I do not have a successor as chief executive officer, so if you come over, mind your p's and q's and do okay—in a few years you might succeed me as chief executive officer. But no guarantees."

I moved over to Stifel on January 1, 1976, and two and one half years later, in December 1978, Mr. Newton told me, "We're ready now for you to become the president and chief executive officer of Stifel."

Well, I was very excited. Without question, that was one of the big developments of my life. I had always wanted to run G. H. Walker & Company, and even though in many ways my first love was politics, I was fascinated with the investment business, and I really wanted to prove to my father and to others that I was capable of the leadership position of a good firm.

I think I proved myself at Stifel. The firm grew, went public, became listed on the NYSE, and I became chairman as well as president and chief executive officer in 1982.

I remained in this role at Stifel, Nicolaus through 1992. Everything was going well, so well that I decided to run for Congress. I ran in 1992 and was defeated in the primary by Jim Talent, who became a U.S. representative and then senator. (Jim later told me that my support in the 1992 race made his election to Congress possible.)

I went back to Stifel after my political loss and decided the wisest thing to do was to end my term as chief executive officer.

We chose as my successor the fellow who was the chief operating officer at Stifel at the time. He took over as chief executive officer, and I remained chairman.

Why did I do it?

I was almost sixty-two, and I concluded, first, that investment banking and brokerage really is a young man's game. The people who excelled in management of these firms were all younger than me. Second, technology was just zooming ahead in our industry, and it was beyond my ability to grasp the intricacies. I was never much good at understanding technology. Since I thought it was important that the firm excel in technology, I believed we needed leadership with an appreciation of it, with an eye for it. Third, I really wanted to do more in the community, and I felt I could afford to take a lower compensation than I was getting as chief executive officer, spend more time working with many outside interests, get involved in local governance issues, and perhaps play more of a role in politics.

There were a lot of risks in this decision. I was not a wealthy fellow at the time, and I didn't know how I would be compensated when I was no longer chief executive officer. There was an element of financial risk, and also there was a risk in terms of my standing in the community. If you are chief executive officer of a firm, you are sought after by a lot of organizations. But if you're not the chief executive officer, but chairman of a small firm, you clearly lose some of your clout. So there was a question about how others would perceive me and about my stature in the community. But it worked out very well. I was elected chairman of the board of the Missouri Historical Society and made treasurer of the St. Louis Science Center, and I resumed an active role at Webster University. It turned out that that wasn't a real issue. Further, I had the opportunity to pull together a group of community leaders (including all four former mayors of St. Louis) who, working together, amended the Missouri Constitution to allow, for the first time, the voters in the city to change their city charter.

But that's not the end of the story. It turned out that the person selected to be my successor as chief executive officer was not continued in that position by the board of directors in July 1997.

I got involved back in the firm and helped in the search for a new chief executive officer. This led to our hiring a promising fellow, Ron Kruszewski. Like me in my early days, he learned that he was unlikely to get the top job at his investment banking firm and didn't appear to have the world's greatest future there. He called me and said, "I understand you are looking for a CEO, and I could be interested in applying for that job."

And I said, "Great. How old are you?"

He said, "I'm thirty-seven."

And I said, "Ron, you're a little young. We're looking for somebody between forty-five and fifty-five. But give us your résumé and talk to the head of our search committee, and we'll certainly give you every consideration."

Well, he did. And the head of our search committee called me after the interview and said, "Bert, you may think this fellow is too young, but I tell you, in my view, he's got just what we're looking for."

So I said, "Great! Then probably his youth is going to be more of an advantage than a disadvantage. Let him go around and see the other directors, and as far as I'm concerned, he's our man." Well, we hired him—this was about twelve years ago—as our president and chief executive officer.

I indicated to Ron my willingness to step down, to give up the chairman's job, just as I had the chief executive officer's job several years before.

But Ron said, "No, I'd like you to remain as chairman for the foreseeable future." And so I said, "Fine, I'd be glad to."

Ron has done a tremendous job. He's making Stifel, Nicolaus, in my opinion, one of the really outstanding national firms not headquartered in New York City. And our share price has increased many times.

A few years later, in 2001, Ron let me know (very subtly) that it was time for me to move on, that he wanted to put his own trademark on the firm. As a result, I went down to Texas to visit my first cousin, George Herbert Walker Bush, the forty-first president. I said, "Mr. President, my wife and I don't think I should stay at

Stifel, Nicolaus any longer. Our new chief executive officer really wants to make it his firm, which I respect and appreciate. We have never lived abroad and have never worked for the government. We would really like to live outside the United States for a period of time and work for your son. Maybe there's a fragile relationship somewhere in the world with some country where sending a family member could be useful."

He listened and said, "That's a great idea. I'd support that. Maybe you could even be an ambassador."

I said, "Wow, I never thought about that." An ambassadorship had not occurred to me.

He said, "Well, going overseas is a great idea. Here's what you do. I'm not going to tell the president what to do. He's my son, but I'm not going to tell him. I don't do that. Write him a letter, and let him know that you're interested in serving abroad and the reasons why. If you want to send me a copy of the letter, fine. Then we'll see. If he calls me and asks my advice, I'll put in a word for you. But who knows what will happen?"

So I said, "Great!" And at first nothing happened. I wrote the letter, nothing happened. In the six or eight months that followed, we decided never to bring up the subject again. Probably there were hundreds of other qualified candidates. It was time to think of other possible opportunities.

Then, in January 2003, the president—George W. Bush— came to St. Louis to make a speech. I was invited to go out and meet him, along with three others, at the airport. He said to me, "Do you want to ride down in my limousine?" I said, "Yes, sir!" Just the two of us were in the limo, and we chitchatted for a while, and then he said, "Hey! Is it true you could be interested in serving abroad?" And I said, "Yes, we sure would be very excited about that." And he said, "What country would you like to go to?"

I said, "Oh, Mr. President, wherever you think we could be of service."

He said, "Great. I'm so glad to know you're interested. I will do some work on this when I get back to the White House tonight, and you'll be hearing from us."

A week later the White House called and said, "We've decided to send you to Hungary as the U.S. ambassador." In fact, my wife and I were not even sure where Hungary was on a map.

You can imagine how exciting that was for us!

In July 2003, we went to Hungary, and I spent just under three years there as ambassador. It was a wonderful experience. What I was particularly pleased about is that at the end of the three years the government gave me one of the highest medals they give for outstanding service, and two Hungarian universities gave me an honorary degree.

So you see where it all led when I decided to give up the chief executive officer's job at Stifel. Now, by the way, I have no management relationship with the firm, except that I am a major stockholder, probably one of the largest individual shareholders of the firm. Another result of my decision is that Stifel's stock has benefited under the current leadership and has provided my family substantial financial resources.

## BARNEY EBSWORTH
### Founder, Chairman, and CEO, INTRAV, Royal Cruise Line, Clipper Cruise Line

B arney Ebsworth put his heart and soul into his businesses. He started with a small travel company in 1959 and guided that business to phenomenal success over the years. Specializing in air and sea charter travel, he offered exciting tour packages to his customers, who quickly spread the word that INTRAV was the way to see Europe and the world.

Always looking for ways to improve the quality of his offerings, and disappointed with the cruise ships he was getting when he chartered them from other companies, Ebsworth decided to buy and even build his own. From there, he went on to create his own cruise lines, Royal Cruise Line and Clipper Cruise Line, which proved to be as successful as his original travel business.

Ebsworth learned the hard way that his companies succeeded only when he devoted himself completely to them. Whenever he started a new venture with anything less than total dedication and focus, things just didn't work out. The same was true when he started businesses outside of his expertise and left them in the hands of others who he thought could add value where he couldn't: things just didn't work out.

Such experiences led Ebsworth to his defining moment. Realizing that, for him, running a company was an all-or-nothing proposition, he developed a plan that would relieve him of the cares and burdens of the intense working world he inhabited while he was still young enough to pursue, explore, and enjoy other interests.

His unique take on "retirement planning" and his foresight in planning his departure years ahead of the event add up to a refreshing departure from the stories of so many company founders who outstay their usefulness or forget to build lives for themselves outside of their businesses.

––––––––

I STARTED MY travel business in a dusty little office with a receptionist who doubled as a ticket agent. I think the office was a wig shop before I moved in. And there were rumors that there was a bookie joint upstairs. I don't know—I never knew for sure.

I did what any businessman does: in the beginning I made sales calls all day and worked all night to pay the bills. I'd take any business I could to keep the lights on, keep the doors open, and start building the business.

In 1960, I did my first tour in England. In '61, I probably did four or five trips, mainly to Europe. By 1966, I was doing tours to Asia. In 1967, I changed the name of the company from International Travel Advisers to INTRAV, and I started selling chartered trips to the Orient to customers in the Midwest, primarily through clubs, including Missouri Athletic, Indianapolis Athletic, and clubs in Texas.

In the first year of our "Orient Adventure," we'd do Tokyo, Kyoto, and Hong Kong, four days each. What made it successful was that we were able to charter whole planes and provide first-class service, while most charters were all about tight seating, getting in as many passengers as possible, and going as cheap as possible.

We would contract for Boeing 707s. We'd have 165 passengers, and we'd contract enough rooms for 165 people in Tokyo, Kyoto, and Hong Kong. The best description of what I was doing is to imagine a baseball game with tour groups on first, second, and third: every time you moved to first base, we'd move everybody else to the next base, so that we had total economic utilization of all the hotels and the charter plane. That allowed us to give a 40 or 50 percent discount to customers and still increase our margins. That's how the business grew.

At one time there was a limit on the number of charters into Japan, and we took almost 100 percent of all the U.S. charter landings allowed there. We really dominated the market. Plus, you could say that I really started group travel in Europe. That was in 1969.

I built my business one step at a time. In the beginning I would go overseas and work out the details. I had a pretty good idea where we wanted to go and where we wanted to stay, so I would go over and negotiate the arrangements. What I generally did in the first year of the charters was, I would set everything up a year in advance, or whatever length of time, and then I would go over a couple months before the first group arrived and make sure our tour operator over there was ready to go, had a hospitality desk, and the people in the hotel understood when the group was coming and what we expected.

And then I traveled two days in front of the first chartered plane so that I would have two days before they arrived to make sure everything was ready and do all the dry runs. Then, if the group stayed for four days, two days before the end of the first city tour I'd fly to the next stop and do the same two-day check, and then I'd fly to the next one, do the two-day check. Depending on how well it was going, I might go back to earlier cities and iron out a few kinks. But that was only the first year. After the first year, we ran nine charters, and I hired a vice president of operations, and that was the last time I did operations.

In 1970 I started chartering ships to run cruises to the Mediterranean. The ships weren't very good, but I starting thinking, *My gosh! This is a great business to be in!*

The cruise business was just getting started out of Miami with Royal Caribbean, Carnival Cruise Line, and Norwegian Caribbean. I said, "Holy smokes! We're getting broken-down ships when we charter—we need to do something!"

At the same time it turned out that we had a tax problem: we were making too much money. One day my accountant said, "I've got some bad news for you. You're paying 50 percent tax on your corporate profits. You've got an excess accumulation of surplus capital." Being a personal service company, all of our profits were going to cash. So I had the opposite of what most people in business have. They're always looking for more cash. I was a cash cow.

I guess the tax business was the genesis of my idea to retire. I was thinking that, contrary to most successful businessmen, I really don't want to spend my life just running businesses. I felt there's got to be something else for me.

So I said, "I'll learn just one more business."

And all of a sudden I thought, "Hey, wait a minute. Why don't I start a cruise line in the Mediterranean?" Nobody was there. The business was new. It obviously looked like it was going to grow. And so I went out and started Royal Cruise Line, built a cruise ship, and started the first Mediterranean cruise line. I built the ship in Elsinore, Denmark. We built another and converted another, so we owned three ships. We made money hand over fist.

On my fifty-fifth birthday, I said, I love what I do, I love the people I'm doing it with. But I want to set up a ten-year plan so that when I am sixty-five—it could have been any age—I do not want to own any companies where I feel personally responsible for the employees. I want to take myself off the hook and go do something else.

That was the start of my most important decision. But I think in a lot of ways that's everybody's most important decision. I always say that when your ship comes in, you don't want to be at the airport waiting for it.

I just sort of thought, *I love this, but I'm not going to make this my whole life.* There were other things I wanted to do, and setting a personal deadline for selling my companies so I could move on and do other things was the way to make that happen.

I have many personal friends around my age who reacted to my plan by saying, "I can't do what you did because I don't have the interests you have." So they continue on in their businesses. My advice to them is always, "Okay, then you've already figured this out for yourself." If you're going to do it that way and stay in your business forever, then you need to figure out how to minimize the number of things that will keep you from doing what you really like to do personally, like going skiing in Aspen or traveling to Europe with your kids or whatever it is.

I did have some other interests. I figured those interests would begin to keep me busy, but I really wanted to see if there were other interests for me as well.

In 1999 I sold out to a Swiss company. I was maybe two days beyond my ten-year deadline. I could have stayed in and made a hell of a lot more money, but I lost my motivation for money. I had built a number of companies, and to me the excitement of that success wasn't good enough anymore. I wanted to find out if there was something else.

When I started the company, we had no revenue—zero. When I retired, our revenues were in the neighborhood of $100 million to $120 million, and our net was between $12 million and $14 million.

After I sold and retired, I moved to Seattle. I built the home I always wanted. I'm involved in venture capital and real estate investments. I continued to collect art—I've been doing that for forty years. I have what has been called the greatest collection of twentieth-century American art in the world. It includes Edward Hopper, Georgia O'Keeffe, Marsden Hartley, Arthur Dove, Charles Sheeler, John Marin, de Kooning, Pollock, Warhol, Jasper Johns— all the great ones.

I have found plenty of things to do, and there are more that I haven't gotten to yet. I wouldn't have the time for any of this if I was running a business.

# CHAPTER 9

# Paths to Service: Defining Moments That Transcend Business

If you are in business long enough, you'll probably become involved in community service in one way or another. Usually you do it because you want to help out and give something back, although sometimes you're just trying to live up to what's expected of you as a local business leader. Regardless of how you get there, community work goes with the territory and can be highly rewarding in many intangible ways—and often it's more rewarding than business itself.

In virtually all of the business leaders I've met I've found a strong desire to leave a positive mark on the world. If their business activity itself doesn't directly provide that kind of reward, they usually find that community work helps them satisfy this important social and psychic need. Just look at the biographies of the executives who are included in this book. You'll see a tremendous number of civic and charitable positions and activities.

There are some leaders, however, whose path to service is more direct. Their dedication to their fellow men and women is the focus of their career, not an extracurricular activity. I'm honored to include in this book two people who exemplify complete and unwavering commitment to service: General John Handy and Dr. Tadataka Yamada.

Most of us don't get to do exactly what we want in our careers or in our lives, but we all do have choices. These two men chose careers of service, and for that they deserve our highest admiration. I feel indebted to them for dedicating their lives to greater causes that benefit us all. They serve as a great example to us and to future leaders, and we need more people like them. I'm pleased to bring you their stories in this final chapter.

## GENERAL JOHN W. HANDY
**Commander, U.S. Transportation Command (USTRANSCOM)**

General John Handy's life and "business" have centered on service to his country. Starting out as a pilot in the U.S. Air Force, and trained to fly its giant transport and cargo aircraft, Handy moved on to numerous USAF management jobs of increasing importance and complexity. His military career spanned thirty-nine years, with almost six years of service as a four-star general.

As a leader in the military, Handy dedicated himself to his missions and to his fellow servicemen and -women rather than to the corporate concerns of profits, margins, or shareholders. That is not to say that he could afford to be unconcerned about the financials of his organization—they are impressive—but they were not his first priority. His primary mission was safely moving all personnel and matériel around the globe for the Department of Defense. He carried out this challenging task not only for all the armed services but also for many government agencies.

General Handy sees a series of decisions he made during his time as head of the U.S. Transportation Command (USTRANSCOM) as the events that defined him. While many of us in business sometimes think that the decisions we make in critical moments are matters of "life and death" in their importance for our companies, that is, of course, not literally true. For John Handy, however, it was.

It turns out that he made good decisions, ones that military families throughout the country can be thankful for and that our nation as a whole can be proud of.

---

AFTER RECEIVING MY pilot's wings in February 1968, I had the choice of many aircraft types on which to train next. I selected an airlift aircraft, ultimately flying the four-engine turboprop C-130. As time went by I was able to fly many other airlift and air refueling aircraft in the air force inventory. I retired with over five thousand hours of flight time in a thirty-nine-year career.

Therefore, it seemed like a natural progression of responsibilities when I was given the opportunity to manage all global air, land, and sea transportation for the Department of Defense. As the commander of USTRANSCOM—the U.S. Transportation Command—I was responsible for the movement of all personnel, equipment, and supplies for the Department of Defense anywhere in the world and for any reason—humanitarian crisis or regional conflict. I also had responsibility for transporting everyone from the president of the United States on *Air Force One* to aeromedical evacuation teams supporting sick or wounded troops moving to the security of hospitals here in the United States.

If you look at it in commercial terms, I was leading one of the world's largest global logistics organizations, with 156,000 personnel operating 1,500 aircraft, 76 vessels, and countless trains, trucks, and other rolling stock.

I've been associated with virtually every conflict our country has been involved in from Vietnam to Iraq and Afghanistan. In this same capacity, I was also involved in Department of Defense support to victims of earthquakes, floods, tsunami relief, and multiple humanitarian disasters all over the globe. The bottom line is simple: because of the airlift and air refueling missions at USTRANSCOM, if a tragedy happened anywhere in the world and our government decided to help, we were there.

There is another very unique aspect to USTRANSCOM. It is, in a sense, a not-for-profit organization within the Department of Defense. Everyone we support gets invoiced for the work we do. The invoice rates are predetermined by the Department of Defense. As an example, in 2005 our gross revenue was $10.3 billion. Out of that $10.3 billion, we covered our operating costs: fuel, maintenance, personnel, and so on. Any excess cash goes to the Treasury.

As a pilot in the air force, you would think that my expertise is all about air operations. Actually, the vast majority of the things that we move in the Defense Department go via ocean carriers. There's a natural opportunity to develop significant experience and knowledge of maritime operations.

At USTRANSCOM, we also contracted with air, land, and sea commercial carriers. We did a very significant volume of business with them—between $2 billion and $3 billion a year. These ocean, rail, trucking, and airline companies, and the wonderful men and women that work with them, are a major support arm of the Department of Defense.

My role at USTRANSCOM offered me the opportunity to develop an understanding of logistics, contracts, and how the entire transportation and supply system works. I was called upon to make countless decisions. However, it's not one's personal knowledge that arms you for strength in these large, complex endeavors; it's the strength of your ability to select people who can do the job and keep you out of trouble! Therefore, the critical strength for leaders, in my opinion, is the talent for selecting the right people at the right time for the right assignment. The better they are, the less the burden on the boss. I believe that the real talent of good leaders is the ability to surround themselves with great people.

Leading an organization this large and complex gives one the opportunity to make countless critical decisions. When the crunch comes, those decisions that have the potential to define you the most are those that involve sending your troops off to a conflict where you know full well there is the chance they won't come back. It is the kind of challenge that has the potential to wear you down completely if you allow it. Although difficult, this aspect of military leadership is also reflective of the blessing we all share as Americans: the men and women in uniform, of all services, willingly go anywhere at any time to support the needs of the United States in the face of life-threatening missions. Life-and-death decisions are a necessary aspect of being a leader in the military. On a personal level, I was fully aware of the fact that someone sent me off on critical military missions throughout my earlier career, and now I was in a position to do the same.

Fortunately for me, and for all my dedicated people, in the four years that I was in command at the USTRANSCOM I never lost anyone or any aircraft. In fact, even the nearly forty-five thousand sick and wounded we brought home from Iraq and Afghanistan arrived safely thanks to the incredible talent and dedication of medical crews and facilities in the air and in hospitals en route.

Because of this particular decision, I have been asked many times: "General, what keeps you up at night? What do you worry about?" My response has always been the same: I discovered early in life that worrying serves no useful purpose whatsoever, and it really wreaks havoc on the troops. To me, worry is a symptom of two causes: indecision (the main culprit) or trying to make a decision about something that is completely out of your control. Thus, my answer is the same each time—I choose not to worry. If something requires a decision, I ask myself if my decision will impact the outcome. If the answer is yes, then I listen to all the evidence, look at the situation, and I make the decision and move on.

It is great to be living in a nation where I've had the opportunity to do the things I've done—with almost no limits. When I think back on my years in the military, the satisfaction I felt in my work had nothing to do with the rank I held. My real sense of accomplishment comes from being given the privilege of serving my country for thirty-nine years. I can look back and feel good about leaving, not a legacy, but footprints along the path of life that people can follow for a long time to come. I have that amazing sense that if I died tomorrow, certainly there would be some regrets, but more importantly, there is the sincere feeling of accomplishment for having lived such a blessed life.

# TADATAKA (TACHI) YAMADA
**President and Executive Director, Global Health Program of the Bill and Melinda Gates Foundation**

A gastroenterologist by training, Tachi Yamada received his first taste of business life when he was recruited by the pharmaceutical giant SmithKline Beecham to serve on its board of directors. At the time he was physician-in-chief at the University of Michigan Medical Center.

Motivated by an overwhelming desire to help as many people as his expertise allowed, he didn't hesitate to leave Michigan and join SmithKline when he was offered an important position there. As he says, "The offer was surprising. I had only been in academics up until that point. But the prospect of making medicine for people all over the world was a very, very attractive proposition for me."

That desire has been the motivating impulse throughout Yamada's career as he has moved from medicine to science, to academia, to the corporate arena, and finally to philanthropy. Now head of the Bill and Melinda Gates Foundation's Global Health Program, Yamada directs the distribution of billions of dollars each year that fund the pursuit of cures for diseases in developing nations.

Yamada identifies not one but a series of significant moments that have moved him along his path in life. His brilliant medical, scientific, and business careers have crystallized in his work at the Gates Foundation—which he sees as his life's calling. Now freed from the ever present conflict between profits and good deeds, he harnesses his knowledge and experience in the service of the sick and the underprivileged throughout the world.

———

ONE OF THE most important realizations I've had was that in order to become a good doctor I had to be a good scientist first. Once I got into my third year of medical school, I couldn't really do anything with patients unless I knew the science. That's when I realized medicine is a science and not just an art. That was a very important revelation, because I had always thought that medicine was mostly an art. That's really why, although I went to medical school to become a physician, I became a scientist as well.

That's how I developed into a medical scientist. The next important step was taken when I became head of a medical department because I figured that not only could I do good work in the lab but I could also teach many people. That's why I edited a textbook on gastroenterology. It was a way of getting what I knew baked into more minds, if you will, through teaching the teachers. Then I joined the pharmaceutical industry. I went to work for

SmithKline Beecham because I thought that this was a way to have greater impact on many more lives through making medicine.

There was another critical moment in my career that happened while I was working in the pharmaceutical industry making medicines and thinking I was doing a great job. I suddenly realized that all of this sophisticated science and knowledge that we have benefited from in the United States and other parts of the developed world were simply not available to nearly two-thirds of the world. There was this huge disparity in access to modern technology and to a better quality of life. This realization led to great changes in my approach to my work and altered the course of my career.

Here's how it came about:

At SmithKline, I started as president of Health Care Services, which was a commercial sector of the company with a clinical lab, a pharmacy benefit management company, and a mail-order pharmacy. They were not doing well financially when I joined the company. My job was first of all to bring them back to profitability and growth, and then eventually set them up to sell them off.

One of the things I did was to sell the computers we had installed in 30,000 or 40,000 doctors' offices, which probably covered about 100,000 physicians. They were results-reporting computers for the clinical lab, and I knew they were eventually going to be replaced by the Internet. But I knew that information companies involved in medical transactions would probably covet those computers because that would be a way for them to get into doctors' offices. I sold the system to a small company in a deal that brought us $4 million or $5 million in cash plus 40 percent of the stock in the company. The company, after it merged with a company called Healtheon, eventually became WebMD. When it went public, the shares ended up being worth a couple hundred million dollars.

Next I became head of R&D at SmithKline Beecham, and soon

after we merged with Glaxo Wellcome. One of the first things that happened was that I began looking at our different R&D sites around the world thinking that I should close a lot of the peripheral sites and centralize many of the labs. One of the labs I was going to close was in Spain, but the general manager in that country desperately wanted to keep the lab open because it somehow helped him with the pricing on medicine that he could get from the Spanish government.

I was pondering this situation when something really terrible happened. GlaxoSmithKline sued the government of South Africa—essentially this was an issue with Nelson Mandela—over its Medicines Act that gave the government access to inexpensive HIV medicine by going around the patents that protected them. The medicine was to be used to treat their citizens. It was irrelevant who won the lawsuit. The fact is that the pharmaceutical industry got a bloody nose for fighting it. It was a dumb thing to do. For many of us who were working in the company at the time, it made us wonder what we were doing there. If we can't make medicines for people who need them badly, we probably don't have a reason to be in business.

When I heard about this issue, I was appalled. I felt ashamed. I thought, *What can we do here?* Then the thought occurred to me that the laboratory in Spain was outfitted with a really good infectious disease lab, and the scientists who were there were excellent infectious disease drug scientists. I thought that this would be a great opportunity to create a laboratory that was focused on diseases of the developing world, specifically malaria and tuberculosis, and make this lab dedicated to that purpose.

It would cost the company some money, but I also thought we might be able to be entrepreneurial with the lab and get additional grant money to support the activities there. I took the idea to our CEO and to the board and they supported the idea. We opened up what became the Laboratory for Diseases of the Developing World in Tres Cantos, Spain.

The scientists did good work there, and they also got grants from the Medicines for Malaria Venture and the Global Alliance for TB, which were not-for-profit drug discovery and development alliances. Both were largely funded by the Gates Foundation. This is how we became involved with the Gates Foundation as partners in making new medicines for treating those diseases.

Around November 2005, I went to the Gates Foundation for an intensive discussion of what we were doing in our laboratories in the way of making new medicines for malaria and TB, what some of the challenges were, and other issues I was interested in working on with them. At the end of my talk, Patty Stonesifer, who was CEO of the foundation, pulled me aside and asked if I'd be interested in running the Global Health Program at the Gates Foundation.

I didn't give it a second thought. My response was, "Absolutely."

In January 2006, I met with Bill and Melinda Gates, and in February they offered me the job.

The issues involved in the lawsuit with the government of South Africa had made me stop and think about my life and my work: should it be about solving the problems of the few—or the problems of the many? This was a turning point in my career and made me realize that I wanted to address and help solve the health problems of the many and that doing so was more important than just about anything else I could possibly be involved in. That's why we set up this laboratory for diseases for the developing world, and that's why, when the Gates Foundation people asked me to join them, I didn't think twice about it.

Now I run the Global Health Program at Gates. During the next five years, we will be giving away nearly $10 billion, or almost $2 billion a year. We've focused on three principal areas: infectious diseases; maternal, newborn, child, and reproductive health; and nutrition. It's based upon disease burden. These are the three major areas that account for the largest disease burden. The way we approach this is that where there are available solutions, we work to provide them and distribute them as broadly as possible. Where there are no solutions, we invest in research and development to make new solutions, new medicines, and new vaccines.

I have taken these paths because I have an internal compass and that compass points to true north—for me, it's about my patients. Is it right for the patient? Every decision I make depends on this compass. Does this matter for the patient? Is this something I would want my mother to have? You have to have some kind of true north that defines your decisions. Otherwise, you're all over the place and nobody—not even you—can predict what you're going to say or do or the kinds of decisions you'll make. My compass allows me to maintain consistency. I've found it to be one of the most useful tools I've ever had in my life.

# Conclusion

When I started on the journey that led to this book, I wasn't sure what I would find. Would the leaders I spoke to be introspective? Would they be willing to look back on their long careers and identify their defining moments in a thoughtful way? Would they simply recount their biggest wins and best deals?

What surprised me most was that their defining moments were rarely focused on heroic feats that carried bragging rights. Rather, their defining moments were about making tough calls in difficult situations, facing up to crises, making heartfelt choices, and taking leaps of faith. While most of their stories ultimately had successful outcomes, the point of them is not that they came to a good ending but that these executives confronted circumstances that demanded decisive action.

These executives' defining moments are filled with lessons for the rest of us. Their stories are valuable collections of guiding principles for anyone aspiring to be a leader. Of course, each story has a unique setting and plot, but they share some important and universal principles that I've attempted to summarize here. I can vouch for the validity of these principles: I have experienced or witnessed them and absorbed them in my own career. If anything can be called universal, these principles certainly come close.

## There's No Substitute for Strong Leadership

I define leadership as the ability to set a direction and motivate people to move in that direction. Sometimes this requires getting people to do things they initially don't want to do or don't think they can do. It's about getting them into a mind-set in which they put their reservations aside because they genuinely *want* to follow the mission. Setting the strategic direction is often an anxious task. You don't always get to make important decisions under ideal circumstances; often they are made in a fog of uncertainty or even chaos. Any effective leader must be comfortable operating in any environment.

We saw Sandy McDonnell's (chapter 5) leadership qualities at work as he led McDonnell Douglas out of the era of one-man rule and shaped it into a modern, professionally run organization built on participative management.

Gerald Greenwald (chapter 1) found such a mess at Chrysler that he had to set aside his personal goal of running the truck division. Instead, he stepped up and took the lead in negotiating the government loan guarantees—uncharted territory at the time—and then devoted himself entirely to restoring Chrysler to financial health.

And we witnessed David Farrell (chapter 5) champion a centralized, strategic decision-making process at the May Company, using all of his leadership skills to mold a cohesive organization out of independently run units controlled by family owners who had sold their businesses to May.

## Ethical Behavior Is Not Just Right, It's Smart Business

I would hope that ethical conduct would be an obvious and compelling principle in its own right—but we all see so many business leaders and people in general sailing with no ethical rudder that we can't help concluding it's not so obvious. If you are at all cynical about the benefits of principled behavior, then these stories, I hope, have convinced you that such behavior is not just right, it's also smart business. For every deal point, negotiating position, higher price, or other advantage you might give up by being ethical, you'll get it back in multiples for doing the right thing and the moral thing.

Every business leader I spoke to emphasized honesty and integrity in his or her dealings. In particular, we saw how Ben Edwards of A. G. Edwards (chapter 5) established a code of ethics for his employees: clients first, employees second, shareholders third. He also installed a management process that promoted candor among employees— so necessary for a company built on trust and honest relationships among colleagues and clients.

Reg Brack (chapter 5) of Time Inc., spurred on by his sense of ethics and fair play, forced cultural changes at the media company that emphasized a new set of values, including promotions based on merit, discouraged the three-martini-lunch culture, and disenfranchised the good-old-boy network that had a stranglehold on the company.

## Always Have a Plan

I've heard corporate executives say, "My industry moves too fast for strategic plans," and I've spoken to entrepreneurs who feel they are too busy to go through the "academic" exercise of business planning (unless, of course, they're looking for money from professional investors, in which case they're forced to go through the motions). I've never felt comfortable with these approaches to business, and many of the executives in the book would agree.

Planning is not about tying yourself down to any particular set of steps. It's about disciplined thinking—forcing yourself and your team to work through issues so you're prepared to either follow the script as it continues to make sense or go off in new directions as necessary. Planning is about imagining the future and, when circumstances change, reimagining it.

It's useful to understand that every business plan is wrong in some way—in assumptions or market analysis or budgets or predicted outcomes. The problem is that we don't know which factors are wrong and to what degree. But as with so many things, the value in planning is not just its end point but the journey—in this case, the thought process required to get there.

I can't think of a better example of the power of strong management and planning than the story of how Al Suter (chapter 6) helped guide Emerson Electric through the crisis brought on by low-cost foreign competition. He and his team developed one of the most sophisticated management and planning processes of any company in the United States.

Consider also the power of strategic planning in Dick Mahoney's (chapter 7) monumental quest to remake Monsanto into a top-performing life sciences and agriculture company.

And Bill Swaney (chapter 5) actually went back to executive management school to learn the tenets and techniques of professional management upon assuming the role of president at Perrigo. He was then able to move the company away from its homegrown approach to business, which had become unsuited to the changing times.

## Be Comfortable with Risk

No business is without risks. Even in the slowest-moving, most conservative industries, there's always a challenge, some changing circumstances that must be dealt with. (Who would have thought that the stolid mortgage banking industry would be turned into a behemoth that could savage our economy?) Changing circumstances usually present risk: you may think your business is adequately positioned in a changing environment, and that's one side of the risk; or you may think adjustments are necessary, and that's the other side of it.

Business is about risk management, which means you are constantly analyzing and assessing new scenarios. I'm not a gambler by nature, but as an executive I had to take risks. For me, my task was getting as comfortable as I could with the information I had. If you are truly risk-averse, you probably don't want to be the boss. Remember, not to act is still an action. As you have seen, many of the executives who shared their stories faced risk head-on in their defining moments: Monty Hall (chapter 4) telling executives at ABC that unless they granted him syndication rights for his show *Let's Make a Deal*, he would not be at the studio to tape the next show; John Graham (chapter 4) personally taking on a lot of financial risk to grow Fleishman-Hillard into a national, and then international, organization; Jack Taylor (chapter 3) issuing an ultimatum to buy out his partner at the fledgling Enterprise Rent-A-Car; L. R. Jalenak (chapter 2) leaving the family business to join an early-stage company, Cleo Wrap, where he would get more control over his future.

## Know Yourself and Follow Your Heart

We've seen in many stories throughout the book that these executives listened to their inner voice despite conventional wisdom. I believe that every good leader must have the courage to go against the pack, or even against the advice of respected advisers, family, or friends, if his or her internal compass is pointing in a different direction.

Danny Meyer (chapter 1), you'll remember, was planning to take the LSATs for entry into law school but realized just before test day that he wasn't following his passion. Restaurants and food were his first love, and he knew he had to give that career a try, even if he confused or disappointed others in the process.

Cedge Barksdale (chapter 1) knew where he wanted to be and passed up an opportunity to work at a larger bank in another city. He saw opportunity where he was in spite of the initially smaller playing field. And he was right.

David Steward (chapter 2) was not getting the kind of inspiration or satisfaction he wanted out of his career despite his great success working at Federal Express. His faith gave him the courage to step out on his own, even though well-meaning friends advised him against taking the entrepreneur path. He believed that he had much more to accomplish—and he did.

Angela Braly (chapter 1) gave up a sure-thing career with a leading law firm to move into the uncertain world of health care. On temporary assignment with a health insurer, she fell in love with the complexity and importance of the business, and especially with the opportunity to do something important by providing health care security to the people who needed it most.

Maxine Clark (chapter 2) left the helm of a large shoe retailer to follow her heart. She recalled the advice of trusted mentors from over the years and started her own company, Build-A-Bear Workshop. There she could create a business on her terms that would delight her customers.

## Take Responsibility

Nobody is perfect—including you and everyone you'll ever work with. Step up and be willing to shoulder the burdens of your actions and your decisions, whether they turn out well or poorly. When the outcomes of your actions become clear, it's fine to take credit where credit is due (although even better if others give it to you), but it's also important to accept the blame when it all goes wrong. I've always felt that the right attitude is to be humble in success and open in failure. And again, if you're cynical about what should be an obvious principle, how about this: when you fail, you're usually going to be found out anyway, so take responsibility up front—you'll look strong.

The people in this book have grown by taking responsibility in one way or another in virtually every story—it's part and parcel of good leadership. We've seen this when the outcome was disastrous, when there was a high degree of risk, and when things have succeeded.

When Frank Jacobs (chapter 4) made a decision that turned out to be fatal to his company, he lost his personal wealth as well as control of the business. Jacobs nonetheless stood up and took full responsibility. Nowhere in his story do we see him trying to share blame.

Lee Liberman (chapter 4) declared that the buck stopped with him when he made the decision to take a strike at the Laclede Gas Company in the middle of winter. In his eyes, it was the only way to regain control of the company from the unions that dominated it.

Ron Shaich (chapter 7) felt the backlash when he made the decision to sell off most of the assets of his businesses and concentrate the full resources of the company on the development and growth of Panera Bread Company. Some board members and many of his executives were against his decision. He was, of course, vindicated when he made Panera Bread a resounding success.

## Never Stop Learning

Leaders are naturally curious about every aspect of business, the complex psychology of work, the management of people and enterprises. They are hungry to know more. I tell would-be leaders that it's not enough to go up the mountain—you should also want to find out what's on the other side. And in the pursuit of knowledge, there is no such thing as a stupid question. If it's important to you to know the answer, then it's important to ask the question. Here are just a few of the executives who exemplify that thinking:

As Dick Mahoney (chapter 7) took Monsanto into new sectors, he knew it was paramount to figure out which industries and businesses were right for his redefined company. He insisted on learning what made these industries tick and declined to plunge headlong into any area until he was certain of the dynamics of the new sector.

Al Suter (chapter 6) flew down to Brazil to visit the compressor factories he was losing business to in order to learn about his competition and figure out how to beat them.

Jim Nixon (chapter 6) told me that when he began attending management meetings at Pet headquarters, he was afraid to ask questions, believing he would look uninformed or worse. As he became more comfortable and started asking questions, he found that many others were also reluctant to speak up and that everyone had the same questions on their minds.

Bill Swaney (chapter 5), as I just mentioned, actually went back to school to learn professional management and then made sure his executives at Perrigo Company received similar training.

Sandy McDonnell (chapter 5), in his quest to transform McDonnell Douglas into a professionally run organization, consulted with many people, perhaps most significantly with Reginald Jones, the chairman and CEO of General Electric, to learn how he would approach the same management situation. McDonnell also read widely and was greatly influenced by the book *Self-Renewal* by John W. Gardner.

LIKE SANDY MCDONNELL and many other leaders, I have always believed in the power of knowledge. But since there is no complete "user's manual" for business, the best way to learn is through our own experiences and, much less painfully, through the experiences of others who have walked the path before us.

I have interviewed each of the business leaders in this book at length, exploring the battles they fought, the challenges they faced, their victories and their defeats. My goal has been to gather and preserve the defining moments of these great men and women, to glean from them the wisdom that comes with experience, and to pass it down to future generations of leaders.

Faced with any difficult business or career decision, you are ultimately on your own. Nobody can definitively tell you the right answer. But by broadening the inputs and listening to the voices of those whose journeys have taken them to similar places, you can find comfort, direction, and inspiration for the moments that will determine your course—and on those rare and special occasions, those moments that will come to define you.

# Acknowledgments

This book has been a tremendous adventure. I have learned from so many people, and I've benefited from their help, advice, critiques, and encouragement. My heartfelt gratitude to them all.

I am deeply grateful to my co-writers. To my son, Mike: Your creativity and wisdom were apparent every day of this fantastic journey. Thank you for your love and limitless time and dedication. And through this process, I have made a great new friend, Dave Conti. No request was too much for him. His dedication, talent, professionalism, and advice were truly invaluable.

My children and their families were a constant source of inspiration. Their excitement, confidence, questions, and advice were tremendously helpful throughout this marvelous experience. My deepest love and thanks to them: Liz and David Weinstein, and their daughters, Jennifer, Allison, and Katherine; Richard and Lecie Steinbaum, and their children, Noah and Jessie; Mike Steinbaum and Deb Dubin, and their sons, Max and Charlie.

To my editors, Matthew Inman and Julia Cheiffetz. Their guidance, insight, and excitement elevated the book and the experience of writing it.

A very special thanks to Judy Allen for her endless energy, effort, counsel, and dedication to whatever needed to be done, often on a moment's notice.

And to several other very special people—my sincere thanks to Sanford Weiss, Ellen Weiss, Marylen Mann, Frank Jacobs, Richard Manlin, Neil Handelman, and Natalie Handelman for their valuable advice, suggestions, and generous time.

I also want to express my appreciation to my literary agent, Dan Conaway. His experience and sound advice was most helpful.

Numerous others helped bring this book from dream to reality. I want to thank them for their help and support throughout the project: Jerry Bader, Barbara Bader, John Isaacs, Marlene Isaacs, Ted Isaacs, Warner Isaacs, Helene Isaacs, Walter Shifrin, Jenny Shifrin, Louis Glaser, Lee Glaser, Les Rich, Patricia Rich, Alfred Goldman, Cindy Lacks, Leonard Parker, Babs Parker, Steve Loeb, Francis Fraenkel, Dr. Kenneth Green, Arlene Lilie Green, Dick Weiss, Sally Altman, Bert Walker, David Smith, Barbara Smith, Gayle Jackson, Harvey Harris, Susan Elliott, Morty Mitchell, Ronnie Greenberg, Jan Greenberg, Lisa Greening, Cheryl Laut, Kim Schefler, Susan Mindell, Dr. Nancy Bartlett, Dr. Stuart Weiss, Dr. Gilbert Grand, Dr. Fred Balis, Dr. Mitchell Botney, Ivan Blumoff, Linda Krehmeyer, Cheryl Leamon, Trina Thompson, Valerie Di Maria, Patti Carr, Barbara Barrier, Patrick Farrell, Renee Reuter, Dana Klann, Catherine Collora, Kate Antonacci, Anne Marie Shimozato, Peter Cohen, Ann Liberman, Bob Berra, Dr. Bruce Bacon, and Mike Kahn.

# Appendix

*Executive Advice and Wisdom*

As I interviewed these exceptional men and women, my focus was primarily on the defining moments of their careers. As an interviewer, I wanted to stay on point, but rarely did I stick to my stated mission. When you get a highly accomplished business leader in an interview, you just can't let that person go without getting as much of his or her accumulated wisdom as possible.

What a treasure each of my interviewees had to offer!

Our conversations often wandered down interesting side streets that bore no relationship to their defining moment per se, but contained fabulously interesting bits and pieces of advice. Now that you've read about the defining moments of each of these notable people, I want to end the book by offering you the accumulated short-form advice and wisdom that these leaders have developed over their long and successful careers. I asked them to provide what they felt was the most important and useful advice they could offer to anyone in business.

I hope you enjoy reading these "advice lists" as much as I enjoyed collecting them.

## CLARENCE C. BARKSDALE
### Helpful Hints for Success in Business

1. Be honest. When you tell the truth, you don't have to remember what you said!
2. Have fun! Make the best of your job. If it's not fun, find one that is. One spends more time on his job than anywhere else. So enjoy!
3. Work hard. Give it your all. Don't be afraid to volunteer for extra work, late hours, travel, whatever (but make sure your boss knows that!). Approach your job intelligently. Read periodicals, books, and so on, for background and new ideas.
4. Don't be bashful. Push yourself. Be confident and sure of yourself, particularly when you're in an area where you have a good background of knowledge.
5. Dress for success. This is a good adage. Be neat and well groomed at all times.
6. Respect your peers and help them. Get their respect and affection. Many bosses size up individuals by how they relate to their peers and how their peers evaluate them.
7. Respect your boss. Whether you like the guy or not, remember: he is the boss, and your future is in his hands. If he's not easy to like, work like hell to like him! Nobody ever lost their job polishing apples!
8. Be persistent and determined in all your business pursuits. Develop your sales skill.
9. Roll with the punches. Life is not necessarily just or equal. Luck—being in the right spot at the right time—is often key to success.
10. Cherish your health. Watch your weight, exercise regularly,

and follow the generally prescribed advice on diet, imbibing, and drug abuse.

11. Abide by the rules. Whether it's the law of the country or the rules of the company, know the rules and don't cut corners.

12. Count your blessings. Remember what you have that others don't and use those blessings for your own happiness.

## REGINALD BRACK
### Seven Tenets of Leadership

1. Maintain your integrity, which is imperative and can make or break you.

2. Have the courage to go against conventional wisdom and peer pressure.

3. Listen, and speak only when something important gets better results and greater impact.

4. Stay resilient in the face of constantly changing conditions and always keep all options open in this age of the unthinkable.

5. Have the empathy to put yourself in the mind and skin of customers, employees, investors, or the public.

6. Have a plan—people follow the person with a plan, no matter how short-term.

7. Maintain your energy, which is mandatory to staying ahead, by paying attention to nutrition, exercising, pacing yourself, and occasionally turning off the computers and PDAs.

## ANGELA F. BRALY
**Outstanding Business Principles**

1. Do the right thing.
2. Do it for the customer.
3. Do it right the first time, and if you don't, then improve the process.

## BARNEY EBSWORTH

1. Having to let someone go is the hardest thing I have ever had to do.
2. The difference between a successful person and an unsuccessful person is that the successful person screws up after they make the money.
3. I invested in a large number of companies in the 1990s, and most of them didn't work out. But what I learned was that everybody thinks the only easy business is someone else's, which of course is probably not true, and if you think you can run a business by remote control, without putting your heart and soul in it, as you did in your prime companies, it won't work out that way.
4. Honesty and hard work are the most important principles.
5. I would describe myself as the owner of a football team and the quarterback, but I was willing to carry water or clean spikes. I was willing to block. I was willing to tackle. I was willing to make the hard decisions. I was willing to support the team. I was willing to do anything to help the team win. I never considered myself the owner. I never acted like the owner.
6. You just don't cheat. You gotta be honest.

7. You've got to treat everybody like your mother. And I didn't hire anybody who didn't love their mother.
8. If you want to win the game, you have to enter the game.
9. Establish the Golden Rule.
10. Don't complain.
11. Expect to do the best and don't expect to be complimented for it. The standard is excellence. Strive for excellence in everything you do.
12. Know when your interests change—know when to get out.

## SUSAN S. ELLIOTT

1. Ensure impeccable integrity.
2. Assume personal humility.
3. Strive for excellence.
4. Foster teamwork: one plus one is three.
5. "Smother" clients with attention to exceed their expectations (old IBM saying).
6. Care for employees as if they were family.
7. Listen well.
8. Focus passionately on your mission/vision—no barriers exist.
9. Be persistent.
10. Nothing is as constant as change!

## JERRY FINGER

1. Being a risk-taker is not analogous to being an entrepreneur. On the contrary, an entrepreneur is one who before making a decision to proceed on a project invests his time and a

measured amount of dollars in completing a thorough due diligence analysis. The result is a well-constructed business plan with an attendant (hopefully attractive) risk/ reward calculation. He will then decide to proceed or not to proceed. It's important to know that you can work in a large publicly owned company and act as an entrepreneurial "intrepreneur."

2. "The Gambler" was a tune that Kenny Rogers made famous, with lyrics I've always liked and respected:

*You got to know when to hold 'em, know when to fold 'em,/ know when to walk away and know when to run.* There are often times in any venture when you must decide whether to invest more effort and money or withdraw—either slowly or quickly.

*You never count your money while you're sittin' at the table./ There'll be time enough for countin' when the dealin's done.* Don't buy a house in Aspen or a one-fourth ownership of a Citation IV when the *Wall Street Journal* indicates that your securities portfolio has had a large increase in value or when someone puts up earnest money at the title company for a tract of land that your father left to you. Wait until you receive notification that the stocks have sold or that the buyer actually closed on the land deal and you receive the certified check.

3. "The Gambler" always kept a $20 gold piece in the band of his hat. He may have lost all the money he seemed to have in a particular game, but he always "had the poke in his hat" and could play again the next day. Never put it all in one deal. From time to time, you will certainly invest in or develop some losers. Keep enough in reserve to be able to get up off the deck and start again.

4. As an operator and investor, you must be able to afford to lose some amount of money now and then. You can never afford, however, to lose any of your reputation. Perhaps you have observed a number of intelligent people who after initial success somehow acquire a certain amount of hubris and begin to go beyond the rules of the game. They inevitably crash in an economic downturn. Be your own straightforward man. You will make some errors, but you will never have to look over your shoulder.

5. Certainly study properly a CPA-certified unqualified financial statement, including balance sheets, operating statements, and so on. But remember: *net cash flow is as important as your mother.*

## JOHN D. GRAHAM

1. Survival can be a motivating strategy in your decision to grow.
2. Always be committed to your dreams.
3. Hire people smarter than yourself. They make you look good.

## GERALD GREENWALD

1. In a crisis, be calm, look ahead, and lead.
2. Speak with candor and honesty.
3. Include all who have a stake in the issue.
4. Provide complete and impartial information.
5. Define the objectives and establish a plan for acting.

6. Respect the team's decision as one's own.
7. Address a conflict with a team member before mentioning it to anyone else.

## MONTY HALL

Over the years I have had countless young people come to me for advice. Having been through many rough obstacles in my time, I feel I have the experience to pass on some advice.

Knowing that life is filled with rejections, I give this challenge to young people in any field of endeavor:

Given the fact that you have talent, you must pursue your career with courage and determination until those attributes intersect with that lucky day when you will be recognized. But remember—that lucky day will only happen if you keep getting up off the floor.

I did.

## JOHN HANDY

Each of us has much to give to others. There are two single things we should gratefully offer as often as possible. They will cost you nothing but will bring you rewards for a lifetime.

1. At all times, strive to give honor and respect to others and insist on personal humility.
2. Give your genuine smile to everyone you meet. You cannot imagine what that will do for them and yourself.

## FRANK JACOBS

1. Always tell the truth.
2. If you don't ship something, call your customer and tell them why you didn't ship it.
3. If there is something wrong, fix it quickly.

## LEO R. JALENAK JR.

1. You have to summon the courage to do what is best for you and your family, even though it involves some risks.
2. The Golden Rule: Those who have the gold make the rules. Having an ownership stake drives the passions for your business. It sparks your imagination.
3. If I'm gonna go anywhere or do anything or be a success, I have to paddle my own canoe.
4. I learned a lot during the early stages of my career about management techniques, principles that stuck with me throughout my career.

## SHELLY LAZARUS

1. You have to have passion for what you do.
2. If you don't like what you do, you're not going to be successful at it. I don't care how hard you try.
3. You have to really pay attention and work at building an environment where the people who work with you can be successful and are where they want to be and want to stay. It is impossible to run an organization of any size by yourself.

4. David Ogilvy had a wonderful saying I live by: "If we hire people who are larger than we are, we will become a company of giants. If we hire people who are smaller than we are, we will become a company of midgets."

5. Be respectful of your customers. When I hear the way some people talk about their customers, I just cringe. Without customers, there is no value.

6. I will not tolerate disrespect toward clients.

7. Try to be passionate and also try to have a little fun with what you do. You spend an enormous amount of time with your professional life and it's okay to sit back and just smile and laugh once in a while. I think as a CEO you have to create an environment where people can put their feet up on your table and sit back and just laugh.

## LEE LIBERMAN

1. Don't make up your mind about people or their abilities before you're really sure what you're making up your mind about. Some people may come across as strong or as not so strong. I had two guys working for me, I said to myself, *Those guys are both good. Which one is better? I don't think I can find out the way it's going now.* So I took the guy who's running the finance and I made him in charge of operations, and I took the guy who's in charge of operations and I made him in charge of finance. It worked out fine. This process helped us choose our next president.

2. I'd say the most important lesson you learn is that most decision-making is important and difficult and you don't always have everybody agree with you. And yet you have to make the decision, and the buck stops with you, and if it

doesn't work out, and you make several that don't work out, you're not going to hold your job. You try to recognize your mistakes.

3. Sometimes when you have a decision to make, you have to take into account other people to help you make the decision. You may not end up getting very much help. You'll probably get some people to agree with the decision that you made.

## LES LOEWE

1. Have fun. Love your work.
2. If you work for a public company, be a shareholder and read the annual reports and proxies. Understand its objectives.
3. With customers, suppliers, and other employees, work with integrity. No politics.
4. Build a strong organization, with potential replacements for yourself. Don't accept mediocre performance.
5. Learn how other departments interact with yours. Look for possible ways to improve mutual performance.
6. When results improve, be sure to give credit to all involved.
7. Take vacations. When you return, evaluate your department's performance in your absence.
8. Manage each person who reports to you based on your evaluation of their strengths, history, motivations, and weaknesses. Don't be rigid—using only one management style won't work. Adjust your actions based on the history of the people you manage. Play to their strengths and assist their weaknesses. Follow up where necessary.
9. Make sure each employee understands fully their responsibilities.
10. Make sure you fully follow the law regarding interviewing,

hiring, and termination. Use the expertise of your personnel managers.

11. Watch competitors and learn from them. If you learn something that is not common knowledge, let your managers know.

## RICHARD MAHONEY

1. Tell the truth. Your reputation, like a shadow, sometimes precedes you and sometimes follows you—but there it is.
2. When asked to make a money decision, ask: what's the worst that can happen? If you can stand the worst, approve the decision; if you can't, turn it down or ask for more information.
3. Bureaucracy often does very elegantly what shouldn't be done at all. Bumper sticker: Bureaucracy Kills.
4. Incentives can change behavior—we learned that with laboratory mice. Incent the right things.
5. Most of the stuff in the basket can be thrown directly in the trash.
6. Good managers manage expectations as well as results.
7. A little insurrection in a company is a good thing.
8. On pay: first it's seen as a deserved award, and then as an entitlement.
9. The worst thing you can do is empower incompetent people.
10. If you can't communicate an idea, you don't have one.
11. Policy is what you do, not what you say.

# SANFORD N. MCDONNELL

1. Ethics controlled everything we did. It is a business principle that you would want to employ.
2. A company must have high values in order to survive.
3. Develop a "thou shalt" code of ethics, as opposed to a negative "thou shalt not" code.
4. A CEO must lead by example.
5. In the long run, your corporation or your job will not survive if you don't behave ethically.
6. People realized over time that we meant what we said about our code of ethics because we tried our best to practice it.
7. The only thing worse than having a contract with the government is not having a government contract.

## The McDonnell Douglas Philosophy

McDonnell Douglas is committed to customer satisfaction by providing quality products and services at competitive prices. We must be a constructive corporate citizen. We must continually evaluate the performance of our products, services, and businesses and strive to:

- As business principles, provide products and services that are cost-effective and superior in value by understanding and responding to customers' needs;
- Provide a competitive return on capital in order to justify continued investment in McDonnell Douglas Corporation;
- Achieve real growth at a rate consistent with the business strategies of each strategy center, with prudent use of depth, adequate consideration of risk, and sufficient diversity to minimize cyclical employment;

- Optimize productivity through proper use of human resources, capital, material, and technology;
- Provide a work environment that encourages efficiency and productivity through employee participation, recognition of exceptional performance, competitive benefits, and other conditions of employment;
- Provide a climate of job challenge and satisfaction, personal growth, and career progress;
- Maintain high ethical standards in the conduct of our business, strictly adhering to all applicable rules and regulations for protection of the environment, and take an active part in public welfare activities through employee participation in community service and corporate philanthropy.

Our cornerstones for success are: ongoing strategic and operations planning; qualified people, properly motivated, working as a team, knowing the results by which their individual performance will be measured; and conduct of business with integrity and in an ethical manner.

## DANNY MEYER

1. Know yourself.
2. Gauge your level of energy.
3. Gauge your level of competitiveness.
4. Surround yourself with people who shape your values but compensate for your technical weakness.
5. Let your staff know what matters to you the most.
6. Do good things for your community.
7. Encourage people to talk things out over a good meal.
8. Say "Thank you," "I was wrong," and "I apologize" several times each day.

## JAMES NIXON

1. Develop yearly budget reviews.
2. Gain confidence by being a good listener.
3. Ethics is very important to the success of the company.
4. When an opportunity presents itself, take advantage of it. You can overcome lack of experience.
5. Don't be hesitant to express an opinion. Analyze your thoughts and then be more comfortable with what you have to say.
6. Don't be shy.
7. Learn your job. That gives you confidence.
8. Always be honest with yourself and with your people and customers.
9. If you stick to it and look at it in a positive way rather than a negative way, your chances for success are improved.

## BILL RASMUSSEN

1. At one time, when I looked in my bank book, I had $17.28, but I was determined to keep going forward.
2. I never think about negative results. I always knew ESPN was going to work. Getty was the eighth company we had pitched on the all-sports network idea. The first seven all said no. What if Getty had said no? Well, they would have been added to our list of companies who had missed a golden opportunity, and we would have moved forward to find the ninth one.
3. Don't let the facts get in the way . . . don't worry about them. Don't think that you have to uncover every single fact and know every single answer before you move forward,

because if you do, you'll never do anything, and someone else is going to come along and probably beat you. There is somebody, somewhere, who has the answer that you need. When you need an answer, you'll find it.

4. Being an entrepreneur requires a lot of energy, enthusiasm, and electricity. If you don't have the passion, the excitement, why should anybody invest with you?

5. Always have an upbeat, positive personality and a good outlook on life, and if something turns against you, the world doesn't end, so don't let it get you down.

6. Sometimes a business plan is more cosmetic than real.

7. Be the "first to market" and you'll discourage other people who have the same idea.

8. No matter how far off the wall your idea might seem, if you believe in it, you can make it happen.

## FREDERIC SALERNO

1. Ethics is very important if you want to be successful.

2. When you have a good team behind you, and they're all of the same value set and all motivated because you're working as a team, you have a great, great chance to succeed.

3. I was fortunate not to be distracted by someone who was so enamored with his own ego, or was so ambitious, that he would take short cuts.

4. The way you treat people is extremely important.

5. People are fantastic when they are motivated. You don't motivate by dominating. You motivate by teaching.

6. I do think that in this world of media concentration our youth today worship icons much more than they should.

False icons are created. I think if I were to give advice to a young person starting out today, it would be: Be yourself, be true to your own principles. Work hard. Put yourself in the position to get lucky. Not everyone will get lucky. Don't be disappointed if you do not. Be proud you put yourself in that position. But you need to guard against those who don't do the hard work, don't have the ethics and the value sets, and then bad things happen to them, and they claim they are unlucky. They put themselves in the position to become unlucky by not being industrious, not having a value-based ethical practice.

7. I consider myself a working-class leader. No frills or things, just a working-class leader.

## LLOYD SCHERMER

A leader sets the climate in the organization that allows people to grow, flower, and bear fruit—or not. What are some of the behavioral considerations that help make a good climate? Here are a few:

1. Everyone wants to know what's going on.
2. Everyone wants to be treated as an adult.
3. Everyone wants to feel needed—yes, even loved.
4. Everyone wants to be listened to about their job.

What are the traits of a good leader? There are many, but here are the four I think are most important:

1. A leader has a sense of commitment. A leader has a private view of how things ought to be and moves the organization

toward that vision. Transactional leaders don't change things much. Transitional leaders do.

2. Leaders have emotional stability. In other words, they have their heads screwed on right. They have a sense of personal values, a sense of ethical behavior, and, finally and most important, a sense of balance so that they have time for their families, time for their communities, time for their jobs, and time for themselves.

3. Leaders have a high degree of intellectual honesty and integrity. When they make a mistake, they are willing to admit it publicly and in front of their subordinates. They'll even eat crow from time to time, feathers and all, and smile while they're doing it.

4. A leader sees another asset on the balance sheet: people. A leader doesn't see people in terms of units of production, but sees them as they are and is genuinely concerned about and dedicated to their development and success as they see success on their terms.

## LESTER SHERMAN

1. Hire the best people you can find. They'll help you succeed and make you look good.

2. Lead by example. The head of the company should work as hard as anybody within that company, and that rubs off on the other people you hire.

3. Set an example of leadership and hard work for the people you hire.

4. If you find you made a mistake, admit it as soon as possible. Recognize it as fast as possible, and take necessary action. People will respect you.

5. One man's problem is another man's opportunity. In many cases it forces you to go in a different direction.

## MICHAEL STAENBERG

1. Return every phone call within twenty-four hours.
2. Always be willing to try something. Sometimes you need to fail in order to understand how to succeed.
3. Always answer your phone; don't have an assistant do that for you.
4. Show up every day to work (the Cal Ripken Jr. theory).
5. People may think you have ulterior motives for doing kind things. Do them anyway.
6. Give back to your community.
7. Lead by example.
8. Have fun doing what you love and you will never have to "work" a day in your life.

## DAVID L. STEWARD

1. Good things happen to those who have faith.
2. It takes faith, coupled with hard work.
3. We are here to serve others.
4. Lack of passion for one's work has a demoralizing effect on others.
5. Stand up for what you believe.
6. Some CEOs are so impressed with their titles and take themselves so seriously that their pomposity and arrogance make people feel uncomfortable in their presence. It destroys the incentive to excel.

7. If you want something done, find a busy person.

8. Good ethics is good business.

9. Build a set of core values with trust and integrity.

10. Manage time efficiently. Businesspeople have time for everything.

11. The minute you become CEO, start looking for a replacement.

12. Winning isn't only about who finishes first—it's about helping others win too.

## ALBERT E. SUTER

After thirty years of working with hundreds of individual manufacturing companies in ever-increasing global markets, my current observations are:

1. Every U.S.-based manufacturing company must be aware of the competitive global market for their products and structure their operations to utilize the appropriate level of offshore outsourcing: that is, employ low-cost-country resources, either directly or through outside firms, including both hourly and salaried personnel as well as material sourcing.

2. Developing low-cost countries have increased their levels of quality and productivity to a point equal to or better than the U.S. and should be thought of as best-cost countries.

3. For most U.S.-based manufacturing companies, an appropriate level of outsourcing to best-cost countries is essential not only to achieve adequate levels of profit and return on investment but to survive. Even if high levels of such outsourcing are required, the survival of any company

is better for the welfare of its parent company than the alternative.

4. Business and government must work together on the issues of taxation, regulation, and energy policy to ensure that government policy is not doing more harm than good to the overall welfare of our citizens.

5. Increased protectionism will not solve the problem of U.S. job loss, as our trading partners inevitably retaliate and U.S. export-dependent jobs are lost. In addition, U.S. consumers lose the benefit of low-cost/price imported goods and the associated increased buying capacity. Encouraging consumers to "Buy American" has not and will not help. The U.S. consumer buys based on price, not country of origin, as Robert Reich, former secretary of labor in the Clinton administration, outlined in an article published by the *New York Times* entitled "Don't Blame Wal-Mart."

6. The loss of manufacturing semiskilled jobs (assembly-line jobs) will continue, due to both offshore outsourcing and increased investment to increase productivity, and there will also be selected losses of associated skilled (technicians') jobs in manufacturing. However, there are currently shortages of skilled workers across the country, not only in manufacturing but in repair, installation, health care, maintenance, and other fields projected to grow in the future. Although salaried jobs are also being moved offshore, the U.S. currently has a severe shortage of engineers and scientists, which is projected to increase over time.

7. The answer to these job shortages and overall loss of jobs is improved K–12 education to develop people who can fill these openings. Our priorities must be realigned so that student success comes before that of teacher and educational bureaucracy welfare. Improved student performance against

tougher standards will allow for increased income for those who contribute to that improvement, and more qualified personnel can be attracted to the education profession.

8. Improved student performance and rates of graduation will provide more eighteen-year-olds capable of entering the workforce and/or postgraduate education. Postgraduate education of one or two years will qualify students for well-paying skilled jobs. A larger pool of more qualified high school graduates will enable more to enter into engineering and science higher-level education.

9. Future generations of middle-class income-earners can only come from higher levels of skill and education, not the threat of work stoppages. Higher levels of high school graduation rates are the only viable way to raise the percentage of U.S. citizens living above the poverty level.

## WILLIAM C. SWANEY

1. Build a company on integrity.
2. Be honest with your customers, and develop a code of ethics in your dealings with vendors.
3. Have mutual respect for everyone.
4. Be true to your word.
5. Hire good people who love sharing in the success of the company.
6. Education will allow you to grow as a businessperson.
7. It is worth all of the effort required to change the culture of a company if it needs to become more professionally managed. Doing so allowed us to grow in size and profits.
8. Operate with a professional management system and an open style of management based on management principles

built around planning, organization, and control, and you will gain the trust of your employees, and vice versa.

9. Develop and employ standards of performance. They help develop people.
10. Hire good, qualified people. People make the difference.
11. Operate with the highest moral and ethical standards.
12. Use a course for presidents taught by the AMA as the basis for introducing professional management into your company.

## JACK C. TAYLOR

1. Take care of your customers and employees and the bottom line will follow.
2. Know your strengths and capitalize on them.
3. Never settle for "satisfied."
4. Hire and train good people and give them the freedom to make decisions.
5. Treat everyone like an owner.
6. Form strong partnerships.
7. Use technology to enhance the customer experience.
8. Manage for the long term.
9. Live your core values.
10. Have fun.

## BERT WALKER

1. Pursue your goals with discipline relentlessly, regardless of setbacks, because often big and better opportunities lie beyond the horizon.

2. Being tough and disciplined in commitment to your objectives does not require shedding respect for others and fundamental kindness.
3. True success is hard to achieve without priority attention to family, spouse, and children.

## TADATAKA (TACHI) YAMADA

1. President-to-president selling takes the discussion to a slightly higher level.
2. I have an internal compass and the compass points to true north, which is about patients. It must be right for the patient. Every decision I make depends on this compass. Is it the right thing for the patient? Is it something I want my mother to have? You have to have some kind of true north that defines your decisions. Otherwise, you're all over the place, and nobody can predict what you're going to say or do because you don't necessarily have a true north. This makes a lot of decisions easy for me which would have otherwise been hard ones.
3. I like to look at the world upside down. So if everybody thinks one way, then I want to turn this thing upside down and say, "What does it look like when I turn it upside down?" If you see things in the usual context, it's hard to see what you don't expect. You always look for what you expect. If you take things out of context, then it allows you to see things you wouldn't otherwise be able to see.
4. If you don't have a novel, creative way of looking at things, then your job could probably be done by someone who's less qualified than you.

5. What you bring to the situation is hopefully wisdom plus innovation as a manager.

6. You can't bring innovation unless you're willing to challenge orthodoxy.

7. If in any discussion or negotiations somebody comes out the winner and somebody comes out the loser, that's not a sustainable proposition. In business, unless both sides are winners, then you don't have a sustainable model.

8. It is very important to be supportive of the people you work with. In the end, you can't do very much on your own, and you have to depend on very good people to do it.

9. Bring in the very best, brightest people.

10. Delegate authority and responsibility. Fundamentally, you can't do what you're going to do without good people, and they won't stay unless you support them and give them the authority to do their job.

11. Always listen to the customer.